RAND McNALLY

Atlas

of American History

BEDFORD
ST. MARTIN'S

Editor
Brett Gover

Cartography
Robert K. Argersinger
Gregory P. Babiak
Barbara Benstead
Marzee Eckhoff
Rob Merrill

Design
Rand McNally Design

Photo Credit
Images provided by ©2000 PhotoDisc, Inc.

Printed in the United States of America

Rand McNally
Skokie, Illinois 60076-8906

ISBN 978-0-3125-7078-1

5 6 7 8 9 10 WC 09 08

Table of Contents

4   Table of Contents

Introducing Atlas of American History

The features of *Atlas of American History* described below enhance understanding of America's past. They support and extend information from textbooks and primary sources. They provide additional links between history and geography.

Features of *Atlas of American History*

▲ Historical Maps

Maps are arranged chronologically. Each map includes a title that describes its content and dates that indicate the period of history it shows. Compare maps of the same area in different time periods to view historical changes.

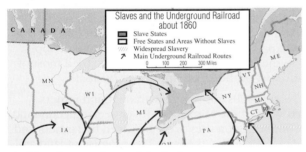

▲ Map Legends and Labels

A map legend explains the colors and symbols used on a map. Historical maps often use solid or dashed lines to indicate routes of explorers or other groups of people. These routes may be labeled on the map. Labels also identify sites of historical events.

Captions

Each map has a caption that helps explain the content of the map. It may provide information about the historical context of the map or point out an important feature of the map. Legends, labels, and captions help tell the story of American history.

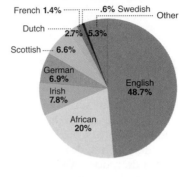

◀ Graphs

Some graphs in *Atlas of American History* illustrate information from the maps. Others provide additional information about American history. They may compare data or show changes over time.

1776

People Juan Bautista de Anza establishes a presidio at San Francisco.

1776

Events Declaration of Independence is signed in Philadelphia.

1776

Literature *"To His Excellency, General Washington,"* by a slave named Phillis Wheatley, is printed in the Pennsylvania Magazine.

◀ Chronologies

Each section of *Atlas of American History* includes a chronology. It lists people, events, and literature associated with the time period represented on the maps in that section. These listings provide connections that aid understanding of history.

D
DaGama, Vasco, *routes of, 1498,* **13**
Dakota Territory, **42**
Dallas, TX, **46, 60**
Da Nang, South Vietnam, **59b**
Dare, Virginia, **9**
Davis, John, *routes of, 1585-1586,* **15b**
D-Day, *Normandy, France battle site, 1944,* **57**
Delaware, **21, 22a, 22b, 24a, 27a, 29a, 29b, 33a, 35a, 37, 41, 42, 43**
Delaware (American Indians), **11, 35b**
Demilitarized Zone (DMZ), Vietnam, **59b**
Denver, CO, **46**
DeSoto, Hernando, *route of, 1539-1542,* **14**

◀ Index

The index is an alphabetical listing of the places and topics included in *Atlas of American History*. The index shows the page number(s) on which each entry appears. It provides explanatory information about many entries and refers to related entries when appropriate.

Periods of American History

Historians may divide American history into time periods in many different ways. Some periods may center around a theme, such as exploration. Others may center around an important event, such as the American Revolution.

Rand McNally *Atlas of American History* is divided into sections based on time periods described below. Some periods overlap to provide coverage of political and social history. Maps are organized chronologically within each section.

1. Beginnings (prehistory-1620)

Thousands of years ago, hunters from Asia migrated to the lands now called the Americas. These people, now referred to as American Indians or Native Americans, settled throughout the continents. They developed many different cultures, depending upon the environments in which they lived. They remained the only people in the Western Hemisphere until about A.D. 1000, when Vikings from Norway migrated to the coast of North America.

During the 1400s, European demand for Asian goods led Columbus to sail west across the Atlantic Ocean in search of a route to Asia. His discovery of a world previously unknown to Europeans touched off an age of exploration. During the 1500s, Europeans explored and claimed land in the Americas.

2. Establishing Colonies (1600-1775)

During the 1600s and early 1700s, Europeans came to the Americas for many different reasons. English settlers came seeking the freedom to worship as they pleased. Spaniards came to find gold and to spread Christianity. French trappers came to establish fur trade. Dutch settlers came for the promise of land. In addition, many Africans were brought to the Americas as slaves.

By the mid-1700s, English claims extended along the Atlantic coast, and the French controlled the vast interior of North America. Britain and France competed for control of the continent. As a result of the French and Indian War (1754-1763), Britain gained Canada and all of North America east of the Mississippi River.

3. Forming a New Nation (1775-1800)

English settlers in North America developed a prosperous economy and a way of life that differed from that in Great Britain. They began to resent Britain's control. They declared their independence and fought a revolution to win their freedom. As a result, the United States became an independent nation.

The original thirteen states stretched along the Atlantic coast. The western boundary of the new nation extended to the Mississippi River. Americans began to settle lands west of the Appalachian Mountains. The national government passed laws providing for the sale of western lands and the addition of new states.

4. The Nation Expands and Changes (1790-1870)

Much of the history of the United States is a story of westward movement. Between 1803 and 1848, the nation expanded its boundaries from the Mississippi River to the Pacific Coast. Pioneers had settled most of the land east of the Mississippi River by 1840.

In the early 1800s, fur trappers, traders, and miners pushed west of the Mississippi River, seeking economic opportunities. Soon they were followed by farmers and ranchers who settled the land. The promise of land and the hope of a better life also attracted millions of European immigrants to the United States.

People	**1769** Junípero Serra starts first Spanish mission in what is now California.	**1804** Meriwether Lewis and William Clark lead expedition from St. Louis to the Pacific Ocean.	**1933** President Franklin Roosevelt creates TVA to develop the natural resources of the Tennessee Valley.
Events	**about 700 B.C.** The Adena (early North American Indians) build mounds in what is now Ohio.	**1565** Spaniards establish St. Augustine, FL, first permanent European settlement in what is now the United States.	**1787** Founders write the U.S. Constitution in Philadelphia, PA.
Literature	**1608** *A True Relation of Occurrences in Virginia*, by John Smith, describes the founding of Jamestown.	**1704** Sarah Kemble Knight's *Journal* describes the author's horseback journey from Boston to New York.	**1868** *Little Women*, by Louisa May Alcott, tells the story of four sisters growing up in New England in the mid-1800s.

5. A Nation Divided (1850-1865)

Different ways of life developed in the North and the South. Southern agriculture was based on slave labor. Industrial states in the North outlawed slavery. As settlers moved westward, new states were created. The question of whether to allow slavery in the new states led to conflict between the North and the South.

Debate and compromise failed to solve the problems. Eleven southern states withdrew from the Union. Between 1861 and 1865, the North and the South fought against each other in the Civil War.

6. Emerging as a Modern Nation (1860-1920)

Within 25 years after the Civil War ended, the process of settling the United States from coast to coast was completed. The settlement of the West also brought an end to the Native American way of life. The federal government sent soldiers to stop uprisings and move Indians onto reservations.

As the United States became an industrial nation, people moved to cities to work in factories. Millions of European immigrants also came to the United States seeking jobs.

The nation acquired territories overseas and began to emerge as a modern nation. By fighting in World War I, the United States also proved that it had become a world power.

7. Challenges and Changes in the 20th Century (1920-1999)

A period of prosperity followed World War I. However, the stock market crash in 1929 plunged the nation into an economic depression that lasted throughout the 1930s. During those years, the actions of powerful dictators in Europe led to World War II.

The United States fought in World War II from 1941 to 1945. It emerged as the leader of the free world, and the Soviet Union emerged as the leader of the Communist world. During the following decades, the United States intervened in many parts of the world to stop the spread of Communism. The Cold War finally ended in 1991.

8. Entering a New Millennium (2000 and beyond)

The United States has compiled information about the American population every ten years since 1790, when the first census was taken. According to the 2000 census, more than three-fourths of the country's 280 million people lived in cities. Americans born in 2000 could expect to live longer than any previous generation. Although many Americans lived in poverty in 2000, the United States had one of the world's highest standards of living.

The United States faces many challenges as it enters a new millennium. It must meet the needs of its diverse population. It must also continue its role of leadership in a rapidly changing world. The story of America is ongoing because today's events will become tomorrow's history.

9. Global Perspectives

Ever since its beginnings, the United States has had connections with the rest of the world. However, today's faster transportation and communications technology means that these connections have increased in speed and intensity. The country depends on trade with foreign countries for important fuels and minerals, and it exports goods and services in return.

1955
Rosa Parks protests segregation in Montgomery, AL by refusing to give up bus seat to white passenger.

1969
U.S. astronaut Neil Armstrong becomes first person to walk on the moon.

2005
Condoleeza Rice becomes the first African American woman to serve as U.S. Secretary of State.

1848
Discovery of gold in California brings settlers to the West.

1941
Japanese bombing of Pearl Harbor, Hawaii, brings U.S. into World War II.

2003
United States invades Iraq to overthrow dictatorship of Saddam Hussein.

1932
Little House in the Big Woods, by Laura Ingalls Wilder, describes life in the Midwest in the 1870s and 1880s.

1976
Roots: The Saga of an American Family, by Alex Haley, traces the author's ancestry back to the African slave trade.

1999
Daughter of Fortune, by Isabel Allende, tells the story of a Chilean-born woman who interacts with British, American, and Chinese cultures in the 1800s.

Benefits of Using the Rand McNally *Atlas of American History*

Events gain fuller meaning.

Knowing where events took place gives them fuller meaning and often explains causes and effects. For example, the map of the final campaign of the American Revolution, on page 27, shows how American and French forces trapped the British at Yorktown. It helps explain why Cornwallis surrendered.

Connections among events are clarified.

Through the visual power of historical maps, the links between and among events become clear. The maps on pages 12 and 13 show international trade routes, 1350-1450, and Portuguese routes to India in the 1400s. They help explain why Europeans wanted to find an all-water route to Asia. They provide the background to understanding the age of exploration that followed Columbus's discovery of the Americas.

Similarities and differences become apparent.

The maps in the *Atlas of American History* provide an opportunity to compare and contrast places over time. Compare the map of North America in 1763, on page 23, with the map of North America in 1783 on page 28. These maps show the emergence of the United States on a continent claimed by Britain and Spain.

The maps in this atlas also provide an opportunity to compare and contrast regions of the United States. The map titled "A Quarreling People," on page 41, indicates differences between the North and the South at the time of the Civil War.

The influence of sense of place is conveyed.

Maps in the *Atlas of American History* convey people's sense of place at a particular time in history. The map titled "Opportunities and Uncertainties," on page 58, is a good example. The map's polar projection emphasizes how near the Soviet Union is to the United States. It reflects Americans' fear of nuclear attack from the north during the postwar period of tension between the United States and the Soviet Union.

Trends emerge.

The maps in this atlas show trends in American history. The map of Westward Expansion, on pages 36-37, shows the sequence in which the United States acquired land. It indicates the westward movement of settlement patterns. The maps on pages 38, 48, and 61 indicate changing trends in immigration.

The story of American history is communicated.

The text in the *Atlas of American History* presents a chronological overview of American history and summarizes key events. It provides cross curricular connections by listing literature that clarifies or expands historical understandings. It highlights people whose accomplishments reflect American ideals.

The *Did You Know?* feature on each section opening page provides an interesting sidelight to history. Like the example below, each of these features demonstrates how history has influenced the American experience.

Did You Know ?

A picture of the Greek god Atlas supporting the earth on his shoulders appeared on the title page of an early book of maps. Later, people began to call a collection of maps an *atlas*.

Section 1 *(Prehistory-1620)*

Beginnings

To learn about **prehistory**, or the time before human beings learned to write, scientists study the physical evidence that early people left behind. This evidence suggests the first Americans migrated from Asia between 25,000 and 8,000 years ago. The descendants of these people, now called Native Americans or American Indians, spread throughout the Americas and developed different cultures.

◀ The Cliff Palace in Mesa Verde, Colorado, was built by the Anasazi around 1100.

Historical evidence indicates that Vikings from Norway established a settlement in North America about A.D. 1000. During the 1400s, increased demand for Asian goods led European nations to seek a water route to Asia. Columbus was attempting to achieve this goal when he discovered a world previously unknown to Europeans.

In 1524, Verrazano ▶ explored the Atlantic coast of what is now North Carolina.

During the 1500s, European explorers who came to the Americas found continents inhabited by native peoples of diverse cultures, from hunters and gatherers to advanced civilizations. Although figures vary greatly, the graph at the right indicates estimates of Native American populations around that time.

Did You Know ?

Scientists discovered a spearhead among bones of ancient bison near Folsom, New Mexico. These animals became extinct about 10,000 years ago. This discovery proved people had migrated to the region by about 8000 B.C.

Estimates of Native American Populations in 1492

Region	Population in millions
North America	~4
Mexico	~21
Central America	~5
Caribbean	~6
Andes	~11
Lowland South America	~8

Population in millions: 0   5   10   15   20   25

People	**about A.D. 1000** Leif Ericson establishes a Viking settlement on the east coast of North America.	**1492** Christopher Columbus lands on San Salvador.	**1587** Virginia Dare, first English child born in America, is born on Roanoke Island.
Events	**about 23,000 B.C.** First Americans probably migrate from Asia to North America.	**1325** Aztecs build Tenochtitlán on site of present-day Mexico City.	**about 1570** Five Indian tribes in what is now New York form League of the Iroquois.
Literature	**1298** *Description of the World*, by Marco Polo, tells of the Italian trader's journey from Venice to China.	**1504** *New World*, a letter by Amerigo Vespucci, becomes the basis for naming America.	**1552** *In Defense of the Indian*, by Bartolomé de Las Casas, criticizes the Spanish for abusing Indians on Hispaniola.

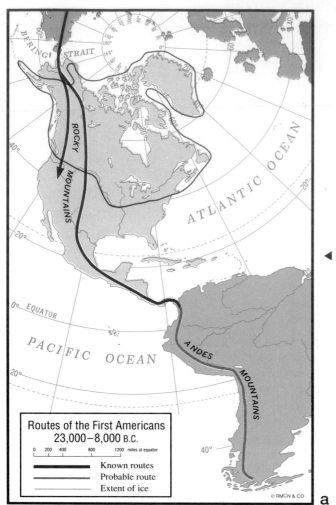

◀ During the Ice Ages, much of Earth's water was frozen in glaciers. These huge ice sheets covered much of what is now Canada and the northern United States. Scientists believe a land bridge existed where the Bering Strait now separates Asia and Alaska. Between 25,000 and 10,000 years ago, people from Asia may have migrated across the land bridge and spread throughout North America and South America.

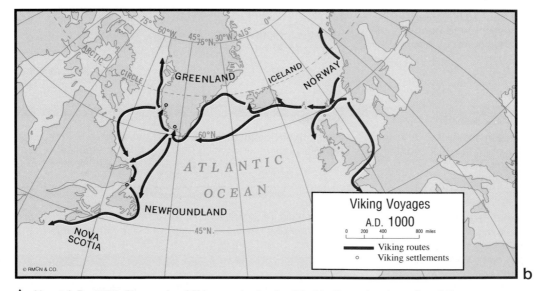

▲ About A.D. 1000, Norwegian Vikings, who had settled in Greenland, explored the coast of North America. They established a settlement in what is now Newfoundland, Canada.

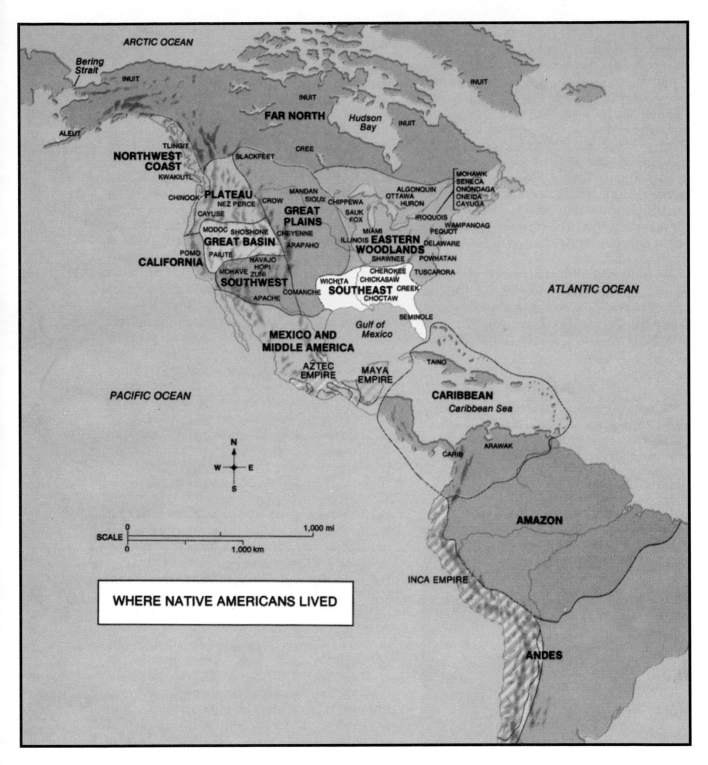

WHERE NATIVE AMERICANS LIVED

▲ *Environments in which tribes of Native Americans or American Indians followed a similar way of life are called culture areas. The culture areas shown on the map existed around 1500, when Europeans began to arrive in the Americas. The map also lists major tribes of Native Americans within each culture area.*

amber
flax
fur
hemp
honey
slaves
tallow
timber
wax
whalebone

copper
iron
tallow
timber

Novgorod

Tver

Moscow

Kazan

gold
iron
preci
horse
carpe
manu

North Sea

iron
copper
lead
silver
wine
textiles
coal

Lubeck

London

coal
textiles
tin

Antwerp

Paris

Kiev

Lemberg
(Lwow)

Azov
(Tana)

Saray

Astrakhan

ATLANTIC OCEAN

Venice

Genoa

Moncastro

Kaffa

Black Sea

Caspian Sea

Marseilles

Ragusa

Barcelona

Adriatic Sea

Naples

Salonika

Istanbul
(Constantinople)

Bursa

Trabzon

Darband
silk

Tabriz

mercury
sugar
wine
wool

CORSICA

SARDINIA

Palermo
SICILY

Lisbon

Seville

Granada

Algiers

Tunis

Mediterranean Sea

CRETE

Ayas

Famagusta
CYPRUS

Beirut

Aleppo

Damascus

silk

Isfa

Oran

copper iron

Acre

Fez

Tripoli

Barqa

Alexandria

Baghdad

Basra

Marrakesh

Cairo

Qulzum

animals
carpets
copper
iron
manufactures
naphtha
paper
textiles

Agadir

Ghadames
cotton
gold
ivory
salt
slaves

Marzuq

Taghaza

Ghat

Aydhab

Jidda

Mecca

Arawan

Timbuktu

Gao

Agadès

Bilma

Sokoto

Kano

El Fasher

Sennar

Sawakin

Sana'

Shihr

Aden

Zeila

Gulf of Aden

Berbera

Mogadishu

Malindi

Mombasa

ZANZIBAR

gold
ivory
precious wood
slaves

Kilwa

Mozambique

Quelimane

Sofala

MADAGASCAR

Equator

INTERNATIONAL TRADE
1350–1450

—— Major Sea Routes

—— Major Land Routes

○ Beijing   Principal Trade Centers

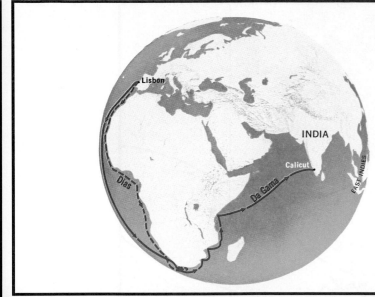

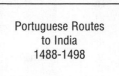

Portuguese Routes
to India
1488-1498

*Between 1350 and 1450, Italian cities
controlled trade through the Mediterranean,
and Turkish Muslims controlled the main
overland routes between Europe and Asia.
Demand for Asian goods led European
nations to seek a water route to Asia. The
globe shows the routes of Portuguese
explorers who accomplished this goal. In
1488 Bartholomeu Dias sailed around the
southern tip of Africa. Ten years later, Vasco
da Gama sailed around Africa to India.*

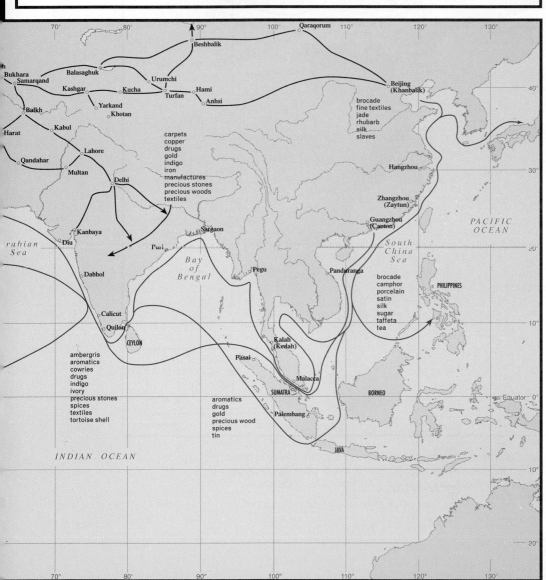

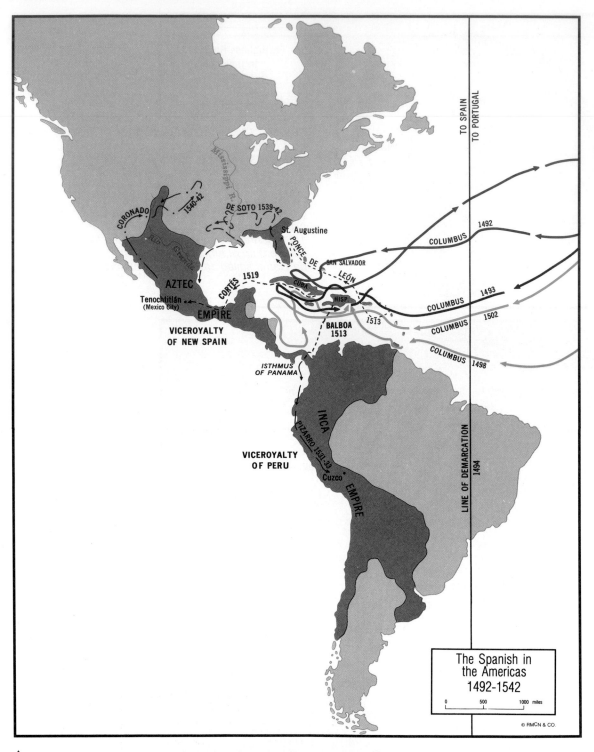

The voyages of Christopher Columbus led other Europeans to explore the Americas. Pope Alexander VI established the Line of Demarcation to prevent disputes between Spain and Portugal over lands their explorers claimed. The Spanish conquered Indian empires in Mexico and Peru.

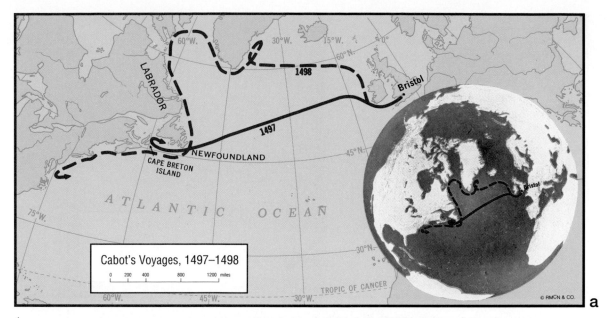

▲ *John Cabot attempted to reach Asia by a northwest route across the Atlantic Ocean. In 1497 and 1498, Cabot explored the coasts of present-day Labrador, Newfoundland, and Cape Breton Island (Nova Scotia). His voyages gave England a claim to North America.*

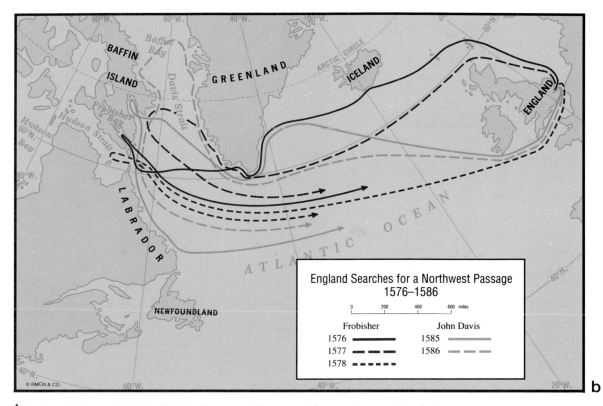

▲ *In the 1570s and 1580s, England renewed its search for a water route to Asia through North America. Martin Frobisher and John Davis explored the Atlantic coast of what is now Canada and the area between Greenland and Baffin Island.*

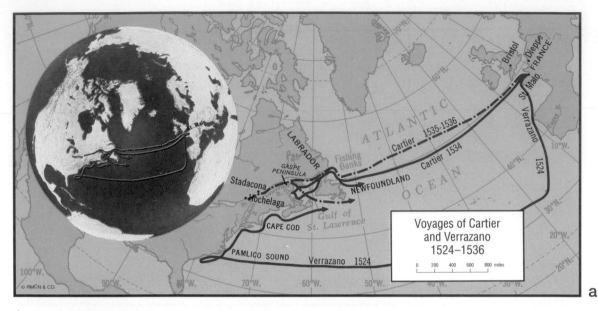

▲ *France also sent explorers in search of a water route through North America. Giovanni da Verrazano explored the Atlantic coast from what is now North Carolina to Newfoundland. Jacques Cartier explored the St. Lawrence River and claimed the region for France.*

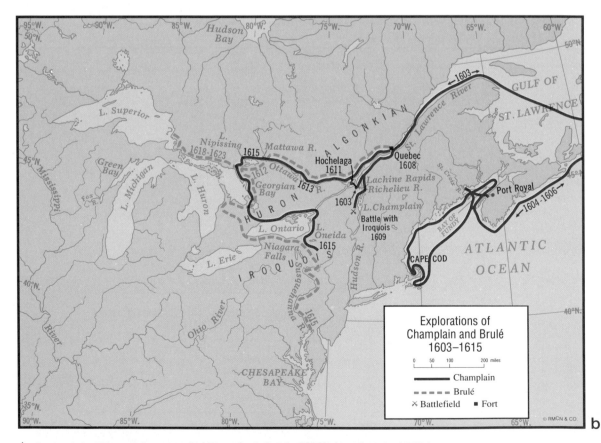

▲ *Samuel de Champlain extended French claims in North America. In 1608 he founded the city of Quebec. He then helped the Algonquin and Huron Indians defeat the Iroquois. Etienne Brulé lived among the Huron Indians and explored the river systems of northeastern North America for France.*

Section 2   (1600-1775)

Establishing Colonies

Between 1600 and 1775, Europeans established **colonies**, or settlements ruled by their homelands, in North America. The English settled along the Atlantic coast and eventually took over Dutch and Swedish colonies established there. By 1732, thirteen English colonies stretched along the east coast of the present United States from New Hampshire to Georgia.

The French claimed the vast interior of North America. English attempts to settle west of the Appalachians led to conflict between France and Britain. The French and Indian War gave Britain control of all land east of the Mississippi River.

The colonial population grew rapidly due to a high birth rate and increased immigration. People came to America seeking religious freedom and economic opportunities. Slave traders also brought thousands of unwilling immigrants from Africa.

◄ This stone canopy stands near the Massachusetts shore. It covers Plymouth Rock, which marks the spot near which the Pilgrims are believed to have stepped ashore.

Reproductions of ► ships that brought the first settlers to Jamestown are on the James River in Virginia. They are near the site of the first permanent English settlement in America.

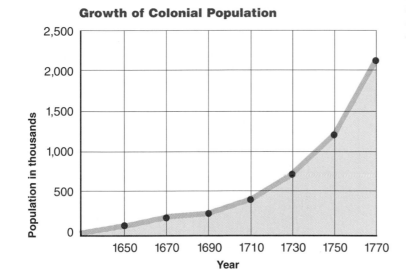

Growth of Colonial Population

(Line graph. X-axis: Year, from 1650 to 1770. Y-axis: Population in thousands, from 0 to 2,500. Population values increase from about 100 in 1650 to over 2,000 in 1770.)

Did You Know ?

Swedish settlers introduced log cabins in America. They built these houses along the Delaware River in the 1640s.

People	**1614** Pocahontas, daughter of Chief Powhatan, marries Jamestown colonist John Rolfe.	**1626** Peter Minuit purchases Manhattan Island from local Indians.	**1682** LaSalle claims Mississippi River Valley for France.
Events	**1607** Jamestown is founded.	**1620** Pilgrims settle Plymouth Colony.	**1754** French and Indian War begins at Fort Necessity.
Literature	**1640** The *Bay Psalm Book* is the first book written and published in the American colonies.	**1650** *The Tenth Muse Lately Sprung Up in America*, by Anne Bradstreet, describes home life in colonial New England.	**1733** *Poor Richard's Almanac*, by Ben Franklin, is published in Philadelphia.

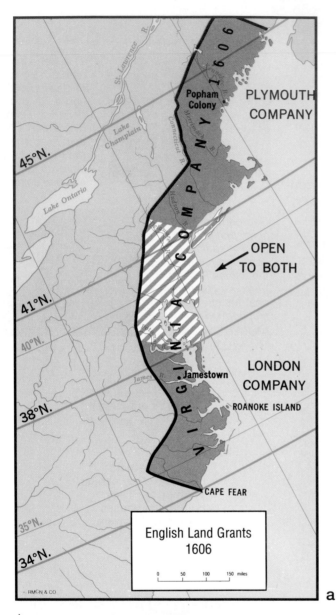

English Land Grants
1606

a

▲ *The Plymouth Company and the London Company were groups of stockholders within the Virginia Company. Each group obtained a land grant from the English king to establish a colony in America. Land between 38° and 41° north latitude was open to both groups. Neither group was allowed to settle within 100 miles of the other.*

The Dutch bought Manhattan Island from Native Americans and established a fortified trading center called New Amsterdam. They established other settlements along the Hudson River and later took over Swedish settlements along the Delaware River.
▼

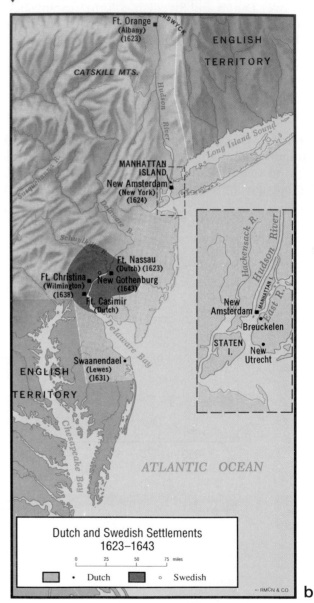

Dutch and Swedish Settlements
1623–1643

b

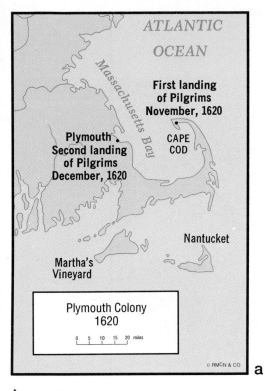

Plymouth Colony
1620

▲ *The Pilgrims named their colony Plymouth, after the English port from which they had sailed.*

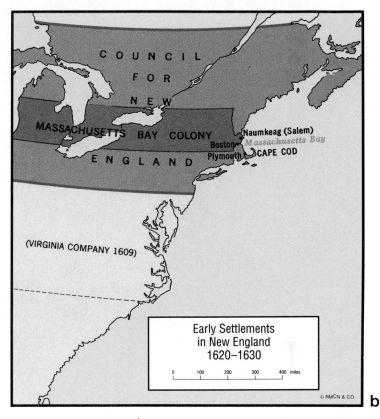

Early Settlements
in New England
1620–1630

▲ *In 1620 a group called the Council for New England received a land grant from the English king. The Massachusetts Bay Colony was established on this land in 1628.*

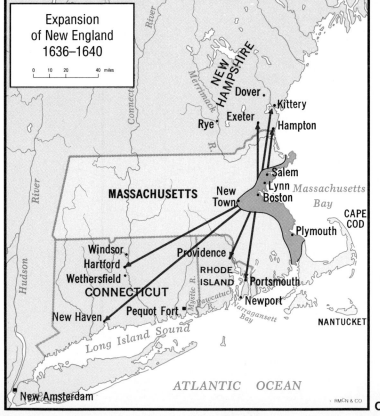

Expansion
of New England
1636–1640

◀ *The Puritans established settlements in the eastern part of Massachusetts, shown in blue on the map. Plymouth became part of the Massachusetts Colony. People who disagreed with Puritan views left Massachusetts and established new colonies.*

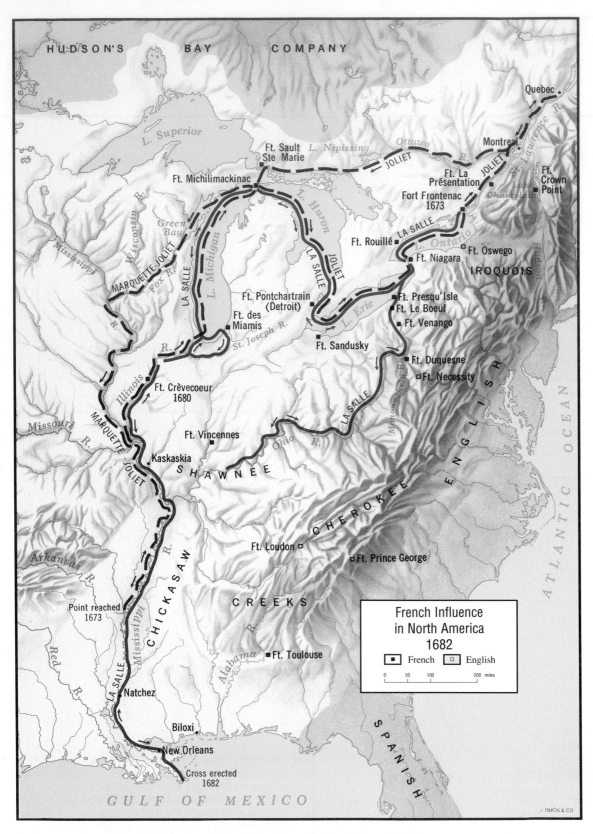

HUDSON'S   BAY   COMPANY

L. Superior

Ft. Sault
Ste Marie   L. Nipissing   Ottawa   Montreal
Ft. Michilimackinac   JOLIET
                                    Ft. La
                                    Présentation
Green   Fort Frontenac
Bay   1673
Wisconsin R.   LA SALLE
MARQUETTE-JOLIET   Ft. Rouillé   L. Ontario   Ft. Oswego
Fox R.   L. Michigan   LA SALLE   Ft. Niagara   IROQUOIS
Mississippi   LA SALLE   JOLIET
R.   Ft. Pontchartrain   L. Erie   Ft. Presqu'Isle
               (Detroit)   Ft. Le Boeuf
               Ft. des   Ft. Venango
               Miamis   Ft. Sandusky
               St. Joseph R.   Ft. Duquesne
Illinois R.   Ft. Necessity
Missouri R.   Ft. Crèvecoeur
               1680   LA SALLE
MARQUETTE-   Ft. Vincennes   Ohio   R.
JOLIET
Missouri R.   Kaskaskia
               SHAWNEE
                                     CHEROKEE   ENGLISH
Arkansas R.
               CREEKS
Point reached   Ft. Loudon
1673   Ft. Prince George
Red R.   CHICKASAW
LA SALLE   Mississippi R.   Alabama   Ft. Toulouse
               Natchez
                                     ┌─────────────────────────┐
               Biloxi   │   French Influence   │
               New Orleans   │   in North America   │
               Cross erected   │   1682   │
               1682   │ ■ French □ English   │
                                     │ 0 50 100   200 miles│
GULF   OF   MEXICO   └─────────────────────────┘

SPANISH

ATLANTIC OCEAN

© RMCN & CO.

▲ *France claimed the vast interior of North America, but it had little control over
the region because of a lack of settlers.*

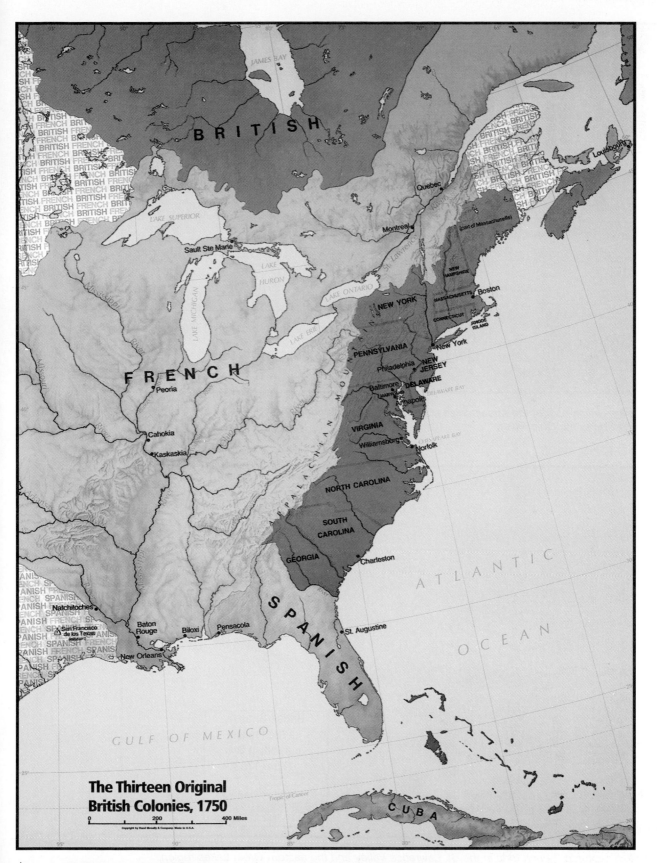

The Thirteen Original British Colonies, 1750

BRITISH

FRENCH

SPANISH

Quebec

Montreal

Sault Ste Marie

LAKE SUPERIOR

LAKE HURON

LAKE MICHIGAN

LAKE ONTARIO

LAKE ERIE

St. Lawrence River

Louisbourg

(part of Massachusetts)

NEW HAMPSHIRE

NEW YORK

MASSACHUSETTS

Boston

CONNECTICUT

RHODE ISLAND

New York

PENNSYLVANIA

NEW JERSEY

Philadelphia

DELAWARE

Baltimore

MARYLAND

Annapolis

DELAWARE BAY

VIRGINIA

Williamsburg

Norfolk

CHESAPEAKE BAY

NORTH CAROLINA

SOUTH CAROLINA

GEORGIA

Charleston

APPALACHIAN MOUNTAINS

Peoria

Cahokia

Kaskaskia

Mississippi River

Missouri River

Natchitoches

Baton Rouge

San Francisco de los Texas

Biloxi

Pensacola

New Orleans

St. Augustine

ATLANTIC OCEAN

GULF OF MEXICO

Tropic of Cancer

CUBA

0   200   400 Miles

Copyright by Rand McNally & Company. Made in U.S.A.

▲ *In about 150 years, the British established the 13 colonies that would become the
United States. By 1750 the British colonies had a population of more than 1 million.*

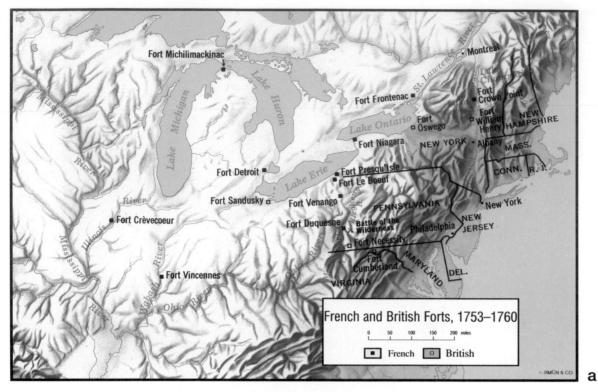

▲ *To keep the British east of the Appalachians, the French built a string of forts from Lake Erie to the Ohio River.*

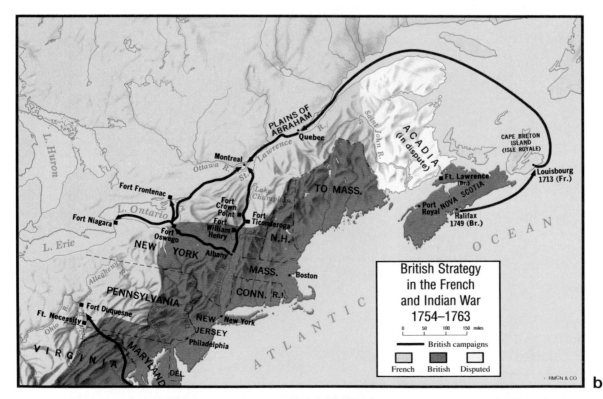

▲ *The British captured French forts in the St. Lawrence Valley and the eastern Great Lakes region.*

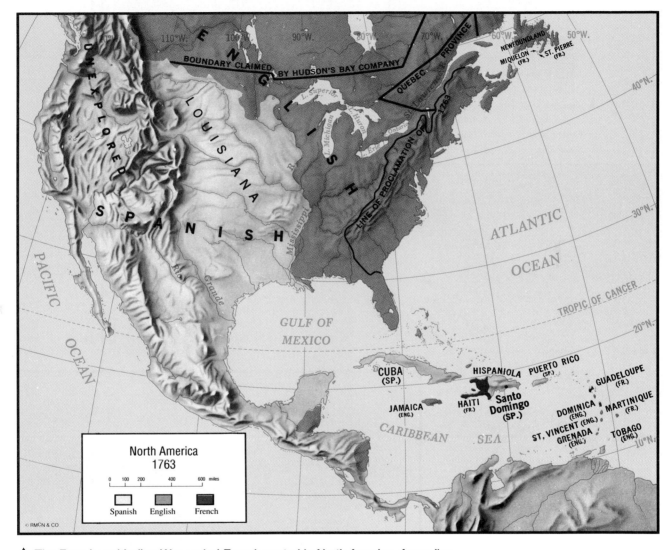

▲ *The French and Indian War ended French control in North America. According to the Treaty of Paris in 1763, France kept only a few islands in the Caribbean. Britain acquired Canada and all French lands east of the Mississippi River. From Spain, France's ally in the war, Britain acquired Florida. To make up for the loss of Florida, France gave Spain the vast land between the Mississippi River and the Rocky Mountains.*

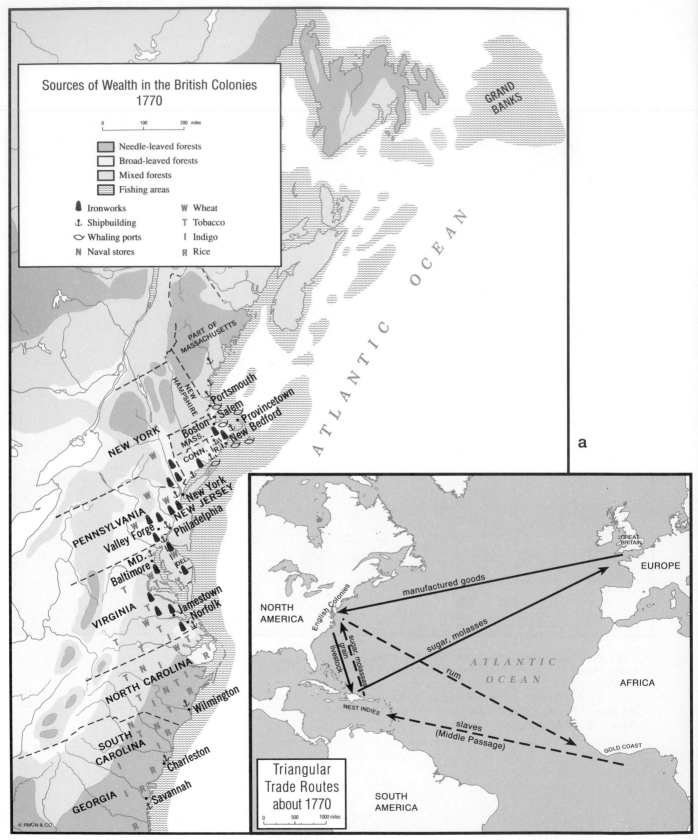

Sources of Wealth in the British Colonies 1770

0   100   200 miles

- Needle-leaved forests
- Broad-leaved forests
- Mixed forests
- Fishing areas

- Ironworks
- Shipbuilding
- Whaling ports
- N Naval stores
- W Wheat
- T Tobacco
- I Indigo
- R Rice

GRAND BANKS

ATLANTIC OCEAN

PART OF MASSACHUSETTS

NEW HAMPSHIRE

NEW YORK

Portsmouth
Salem
Boston
MASS.
CONN.
R.I.
Provincetown
New Bedford

NEW JERSEY
New York
PENNSYLVANIA
Valley Forge
Philadelphia
MD.
Baltimore
DEL

VIRGINIA
Jamestown
Norfolk

NORTH CAROLINA
Wilmington

SOUTH CAROLINA
Charleston

GEORGIA
Savannah

© RMCN & CO

a

Triangular Trade Routes about 1770

0   500   1000 miles

NORTH AMERICA
English Colonies
manufactured goods
sugar, molasses
rum
GREAT BRITAIN
EUROPE

sugar, molasses
grain, livestock
WEST INDIES

ATLANTIC OCEAN

AFRICA

slaves (Middle Passage)
GOLD COAST

SOUTH AMERICA

b

▲ *Some colonial trade involved the exchange of goods for slaves. Thousands of unwilling immigrants from Africa suffered terribly during the voyage to America.*

Section 3   *(1775-1800)*

Forming a New Nation

Between 1775 and 1800, the United States became an independent nation and established a new government. The Revolutionary War began when American minutemen clashed with British soldiers at Lexington and Concord in 1775. It ended in 1781 when Washington's troops, aided by French forces, defeated Cornwallis and his British troops at Yorktown.

The Treaty of Paris of 1783 recognized the independence of the United States and established its borders. The nation extended from the Atlantic Coast to the Mississippi River. The new states **ceded**, or gave up, their western lands to the federal government. The government created the Northwest Territory and provided for the sale of land to settlers.

The Constitution, ratified in 1788, established the government that remains in effect today. The census in 1790 indicated the national origins of the American population.

◄ *This statue in Boston honors Paul Revere's historic ride on April 18, 1775. Revere rode from Boston to Lexington to warn colonists that the British were coming. During the 1700s,*

Spaniards built missions, like the one shown here, throughout the southwestern part of the present United States. ▶

Population by National Origin, 1790

French **1.4%**   **.6%** Swedish
Dutch   **2.7%** **5.3%**   Other
Scottish **6.6%**
German **6.9%**
Irish **7.8%**
African **20%**
English **48.7%**

Did You Know?

The states carved from the Northwest Territory might be different if Thomas Jefferson had named them. He suggested such names as Dolypotamia, Assinisippia, and Metropotamia.

	1776	1789	1791
People	Juan Bautista de Anza establishes a presidio at San Francisco.	George Washington takes presidential oath of office in New York.	Benjamin Banneker, an African American surveyor, helps plan Washington, D.C.

	1776	1785	1800
Events	Declaration of Independence is signed in Philadelphia.	Land Ordinance provides plan for sale of land in the Northwest Territory.	Washington, D.C. becomes the national capital.

	1776	1782	1787
Literature	"To His Excellency, General Washington," by a slave named Phillis Wheatley, is printed in the Pennsylvania Magazine.	*Letters from an American Farmer*, by Jean de Crèvecoeur, describes social customs in the United States.	*The Federalist*, by Hamilton, Madison, and Jay, urges New York to ratify the Constitution.

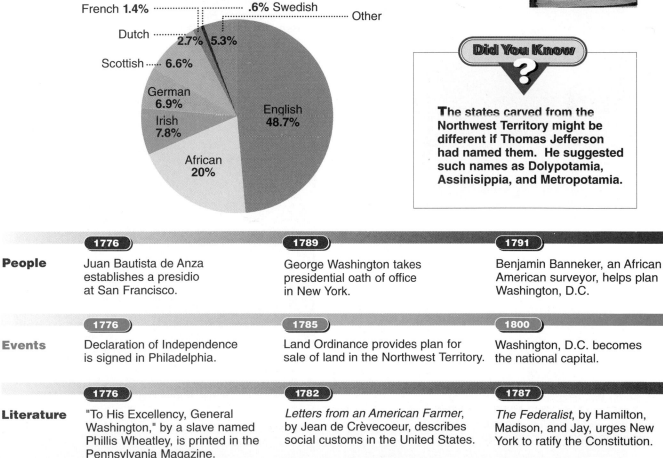

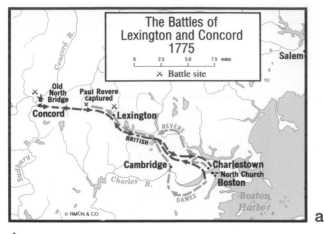

The Battles of
Lexington and Concord
1775

0   2.5   5.0   7.5 miles

✕ Battle site

▲ On the way to Concord, the British were met
at Lexington by minutemen who had been
warned by William Dawes and Paul Revere.

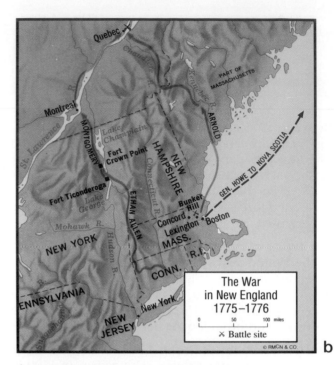

The War
in New England
1775–1776

0   50   100 miles

✕ Battle site

▲ Americans captured British artillery at
Forts Ticonderoga and Crown Point. They
used the cannons in Boston, where they
forced General William Howe and his troops
to leave. An American invasion of Canada,
led by General Richard Montgomery and
Benedict Arnold, failed.

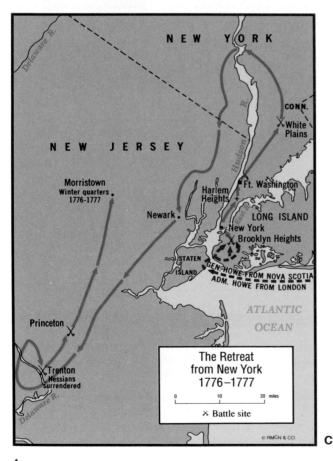

The Retreat
from New York
1776–1777

0   10   20 miles

✕ Battle site

▲ The British victory on Long Island forced
George Washington and his troops to
retreat from New York. After victories at
Trenton and Princeton, American troops
moved to winter quarters at Morristown.

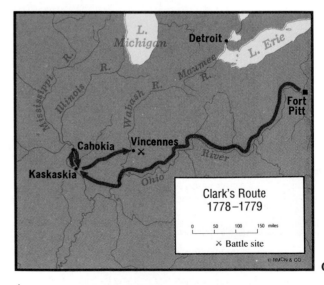

Clark's Route
1778–1779

0   50   100   150 miles

✕ Battle site

▲ Troops led by George Rogers Clark captured
British settlements in the Ohio Valley.

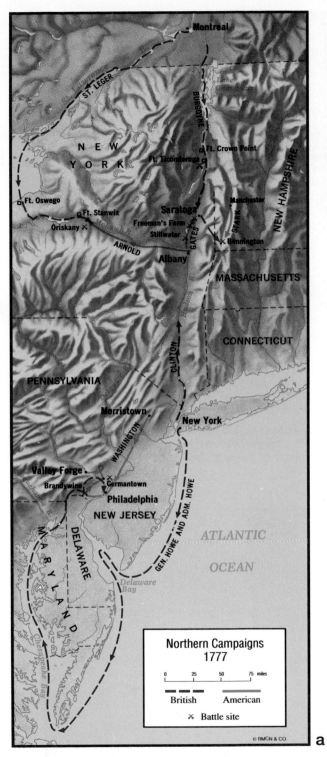

Northern Campaigns
1777

0   25   50   75 miles

British   American
✕ Battle site

© RMCN & CO.

a

▲ Americans suffered heavy losses at
Philadelphia and Germantown, but their
victory at Saratoga convinced France to
enter the war on the American side.

The War in the South
1780–1781

0   50   100 miles

British   American
✕ Battle site

© RMCN & CO.

b

▲ British troops sailed to major ports in the South.

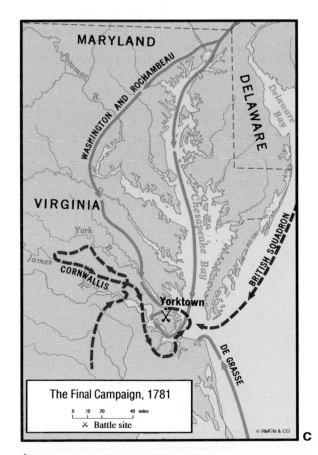

The Final Campaign, 1781

0 10 20   40 miles

✕ Battle site

© RMCN & CO.

c

▲ The war ended at Yorktown when
General Charles Cornwallis and his
troops surrendered.

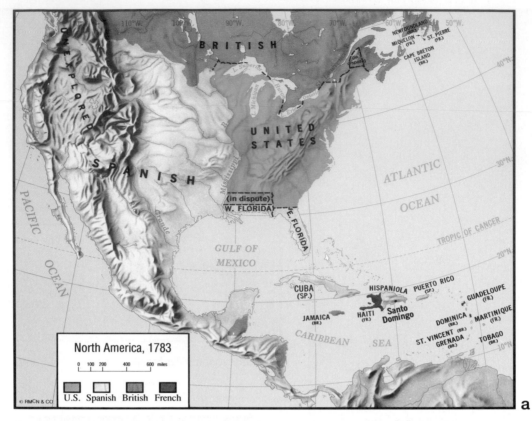

▲ The Treaty of Paris of 1783 established the boundaries of the United States. The new nation extended from the Atlantic Ocean to the Mississippi River and from 31° north latitude to the Canadian border. The treaty granted Florida to Spain.

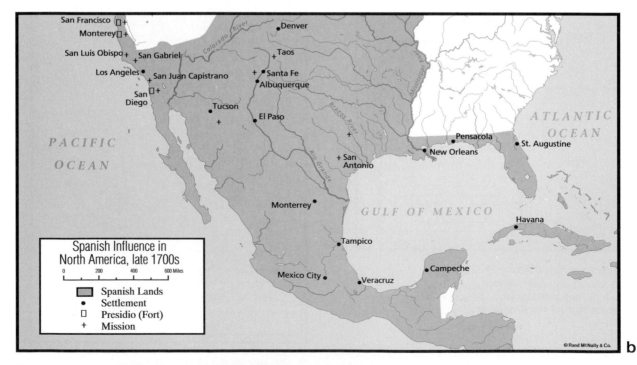

▲ Spaniards established forts to protect their lands and missions to spread their faith.

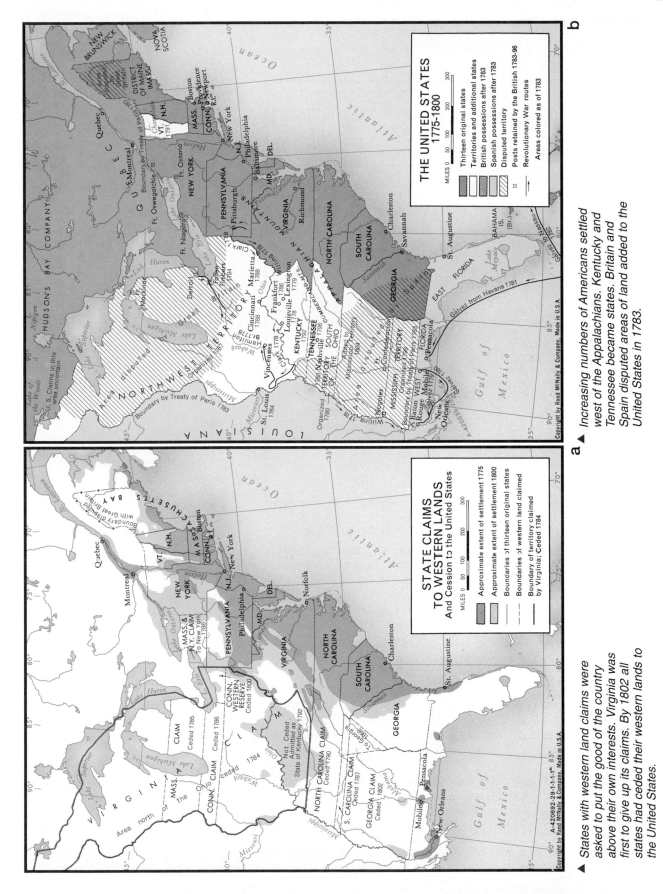

b

▲ Increasing numbers of Americans settled west of the Appalachians. Kentucky and Tennessee became states. Britain and Spain disputed areas of land added to the United States in 1783.

a ▲

▲ States with western land claims were asked to put the good of the country above their own interests. Virginia was first to give up its claims. By 1802 all states had ceded their western lands to the United States.

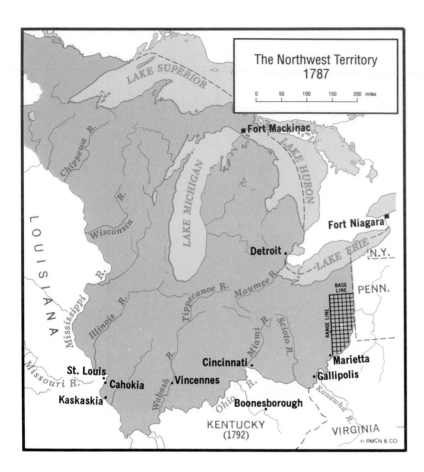

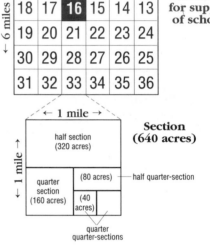

The Northwest Territory was land north of the Ohio River that later became the states of Ohio, Indiana, Illinois, Michigan, and Wisconsin. The Land Ordinance of 1785 provided a plan for the sale of this land.

Public lands were divided into townships that were six miles square. Each township was divided into 36 sections, as shown on the diagram. Each section consisted of 640 acres, and it sold for $1 per acre. The small white square in the grid on the map represents one township.

In the 1780s, few settlers could afford to buy a section of land. Companies such as the Ohio Company and Scioto Company bought land from the government and divided it into smaller lots. Then they sold it to settlers at a profit.

Section 16 in each township was set aside by the government for the support of education. Settlers could rent or sell this land to raise money for public schools.

Section 4 (1790-1870)

The Nation Expands & Changes

Between 1790 and 1870, the United States expanded its boundaries to the Pacific Coast. Through the Louisiana Purchase in 1803, it acquired the vast land between the Mississippi River and the Rocky Mountains. Through war with Mexico, 1846-1848, it gained land in the Southwest. Through a treaty with Britain in 1846, it gained land in the Pacific Northwest. Within 70 years after the United States became an independent nation, it had tripled in size.

Explorers, trappers, and traders blazed trails to the West. Pioneers rapidly settled new territories, pushing the **frontier**, or edge of settled land, west of the Mississippi River. Settlers followed the Oregon Trail to the Pacific Northwest. Mormons traveled to Utah in search of religious freedom. Gold seekers poured into California. Millions of immigrants from Europe came to the United States seeking a better life.

The Gateway Arch stands along the Mississippi River in St. Louis. It honors the Louisiana Purchase and the pioneers who settled the West.

This monument marks the Oregon Trail, which thousands of pioneers traveled from Independence, Missouri, to the Oregon country.

Did You Know?

Francis Scott Key wrote "The Star-Spangled Banner" during the War of 1812 as he watched the bombardment of Fort McHenry from a ship in Baltimore Harbor. The words were set to music and later became our national anthem.

Area of Selected Lands Added to the United States, 1803-1867

Year		Millions of acres
1803	Louisiana Purchase	~520
1845	Texas Annexation	~250
1846	Oregon Treaty	~180
1848	Mexican Cession	~330
1867	Alaska Purchase	~370

(scale: 0 200 400 600)

People

1803 President Thomas Jefferson purchases Louisiana Territory from France.

1847 Brigham Young leads Mormon migration from Illinois to the Great Salt Lake.

1848 Elizabeth Cady Stanton and Lucretia Mott hold women's rights convention in New York.

Events

1819 United States acquires Florida from Spain.

1825 Erie Canal links the Great Lakes and Atlantic Ocean.

1849 Gold rush brings thousands of people to California.

Literature

1820 "Rip Van Winkle," by Washington Irving, is set in the Catskill Mountains.

1827 *The Prairie*, by James Fenimore Cooper, describes frontier life on the western plains.

1854 *Walden*, by Henry David Thoreau, describes the beauty of nature in Massachusetts.

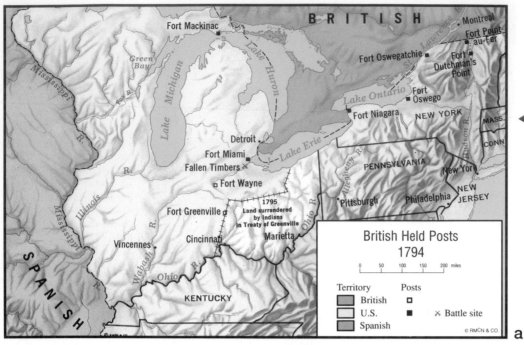

◀ *The British violated the Treaty of Paris of 1783 by keeping posts in U.S. territory.*

British Held Posts 1794

0 50 100 150 200 miles

Territory	Posts
British	□
U.S.	■
Spanish	✕ Battle site

© RMCN & CO.

a

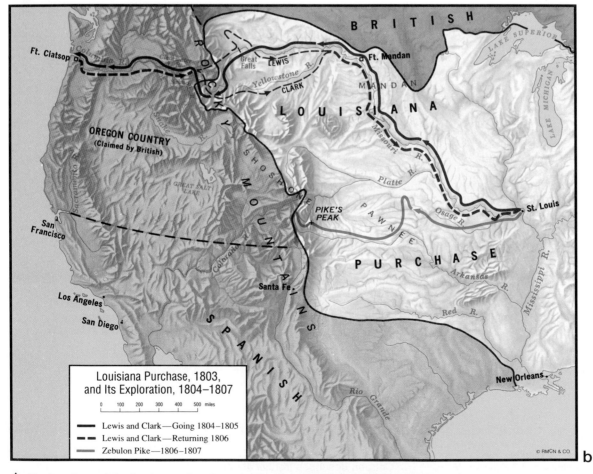

Louisiana Purchase, 1803, and Its Exploration, 1804–1807

0 100 200 300 400 500 miles

── Lewis and Clark—Going 1804–1805
- - - Lewis and Clark—Returning 1806
── Zebulon Pike—1806–1807

© RMCN & CO.

b

▲ *Explorations of the Louisiana Purchase by Lewis and Clark and Pike provided valuable information about lands west of the Mississippi River.*

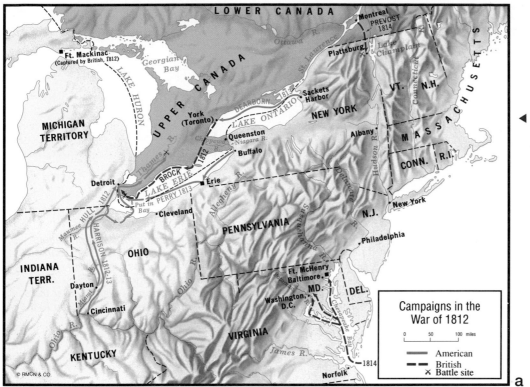

Campaigns in the War of 1812 were widely scattered. They included a decisive U.S. victory on Lake Erie as well as the British capture and burning of Washington, D.C.

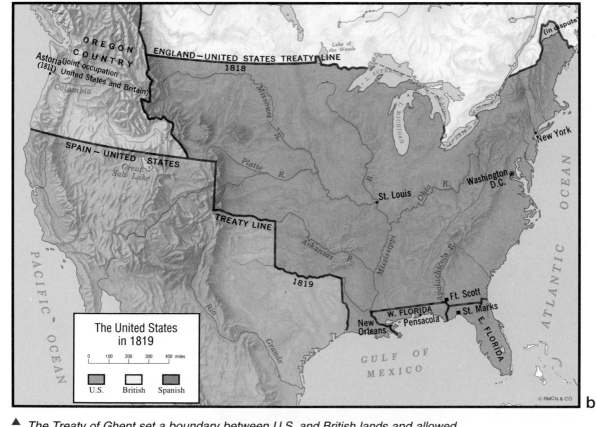

The Treaty of Ghent set a boundary between U.S. and British lands and allowed both nations to settle the Oregon Country. The Adams-Onís Treaty set a boundary between U.S. and Spanish lands and gave Florida to the United States.

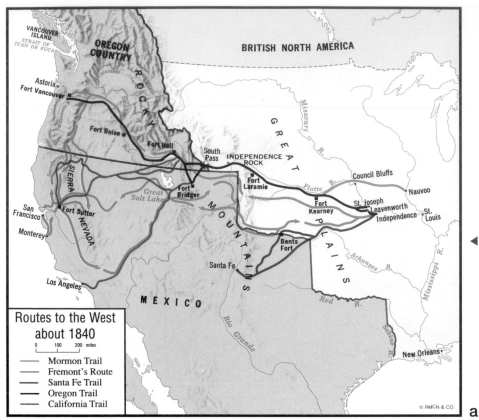

◀ The constant traffic of settlers to the Oregon Country marked a trail across the Great Plains and Rocky Mountains. Traders and trappers blazed other trails that settlers later followed to the Far West.

a

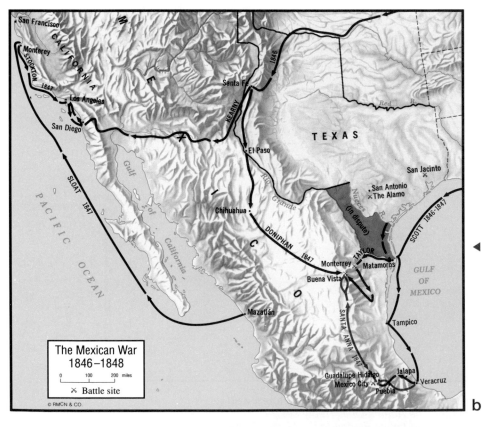

◀ The Mexican War began with a dispute over the southern boundary of Texas—the area shown in pink on the map. It ended when General Winfield Scott defeated Santa Anna and captured Mexico City. As a result of this war, the United States gained a large territory in the southwest.

b

35

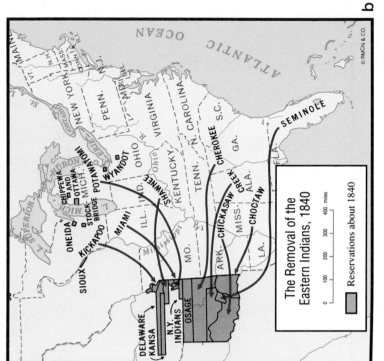

The Removal of the
Eastern Indians, 1840

Reservations about 1840

0 100 200 300 400 miles

▲ The U.S. government forced Native
Americans to leave their lands in the
East and move to reservations in the
West. The journey of 15,000 Cherokees
from Georgia to Oklahoma became
known as the Trail of Tears. About 4,000
Indians died along the way.

b

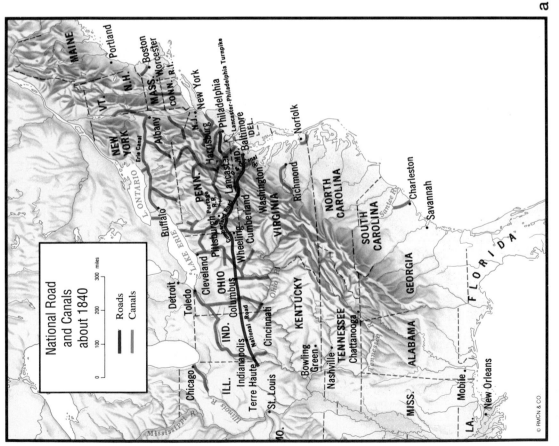

National Road
and Canals
about 1840

Roads
Canals

0 100 200 300 miles

▲ The Cumberland Road, also called the
National Road, extended from Maryland
to Illinois. The Erie Canal provided a
link between the Great Lakes and the
Atlantic Ocean.

a

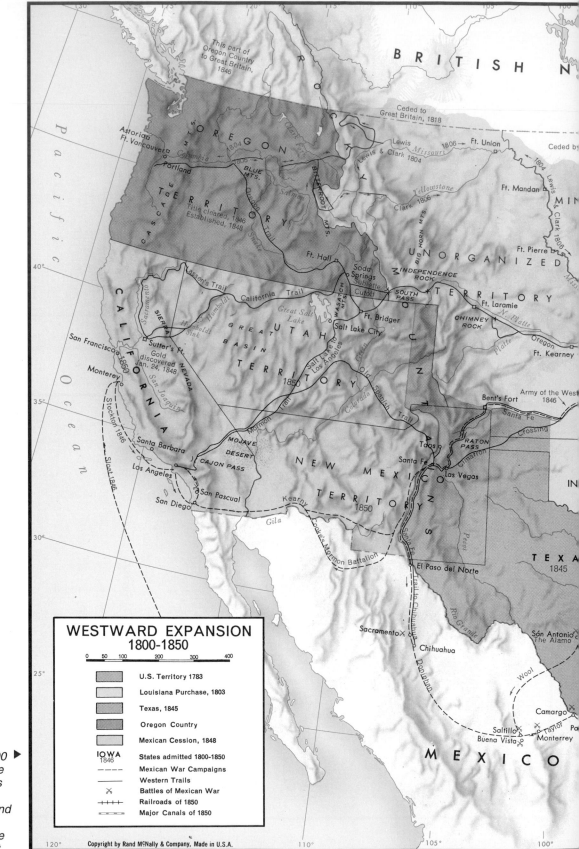

Between 1800 ▶
and 1850, the
United States
added fifteen
new states and
extended its
borders to the
Pacific Coast.

WESTWARD EXPANSION
1800-1850

0   50 100   200   300   400

	U.S. Territory 1783
	Louisiana Purchase, 1803
	Texas, 1845
	Oregon Country
	Mexican Cession, 1848
IOWA 1846	States admitted 1800-1850
– – –	Mexican War Campaigns
———	Western Trails
✕	Battles of Mexican War
+++++	Railroads of 1850
═══	Major Canals of 1850

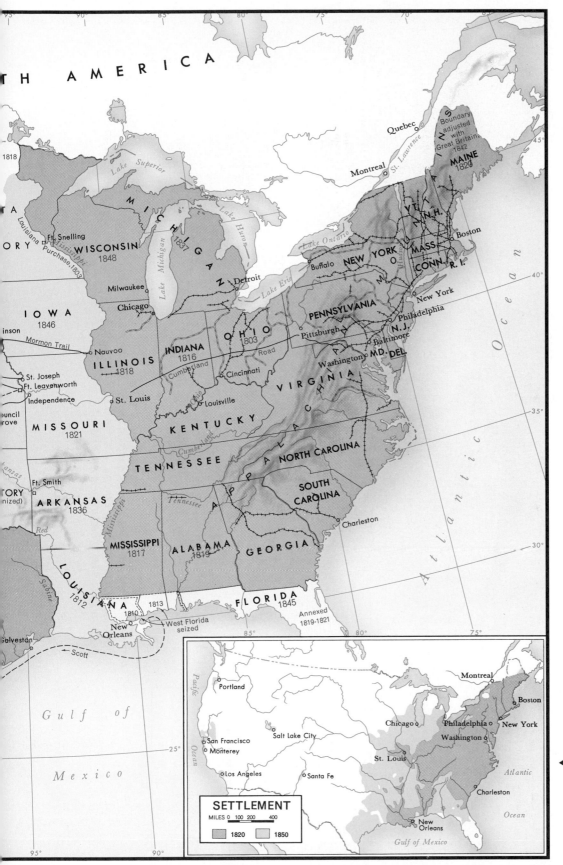

NORTH AMERICA

1818

Ft. Snelling
Louisiana Purchase,1803
Mississippi

WISCONSIN
1848

MICHIGAN
1837

Lake Superior

Lake Michigan

Lake Huron

Quebec

Montreal

St. Lawrence

Boundary
adjusted
with
Great Britain,
1842

MAINE
1820

VT.
N.H.
MASS.
CONN.
R.I.

Lake Ontario

Milwaukee

Chicago

Detroit

Lake Erie

Buffalo

NEW YORK

New York

IOWA
1846

Mormon Trail

Nauvoo

ILLINOIS
1818

INDIANA
1816

OHIO
1803

Cumberland Road

PENNSYLVANIA

Pittsburgh

Philadelphia

N.J.

Baltimore

MD. DEL.

Washington

VIRGINIA

St. Joseph

Ft. Leavenworth

Independence

Council Grove

St. Louis

Cincinnati

Louisville

KENTUCKY

Hudson

Atlantic Ocean

45°

40°

35°

MISSOURI
1821

TENNESSEE

Cumberland

NORTH CAROLINA

APPALACHIAN

Ft. Smith

ARKANSAS
1836

TERRITORY
(organized)

Red

Tennessee

SOUTH
CAROLINA

Charleston

MISSISSIPPI
1817

ALABAMA
1819

GEORGIA

LOUISIANA
1812

1810

West Florida
seized

1813

FLORIDA
1845

Annexed
1819-1821

30°

New
Orleans

Galveston

Scott

Gulf of Mexico

Sabine

95°

90°

85°

80°

75°

SETTLEMENT

MILES 0 100 200 400

1820   1850

Portland

San Francisco

Monterey

Los Angeles

Salt Lake City

Santa Fe

St. Louis

Chicago

Montreal

Boston

Philadelphia   New York

Washington

Charleston

New
Orleans

Pacific Ocean

Atlantic Ocean

Gulf of Mexico

25°

*◀ By 1850
settlement had
spread west of
the Mississippi
River. Thousands
of settlers also
moved to the
Far West.*

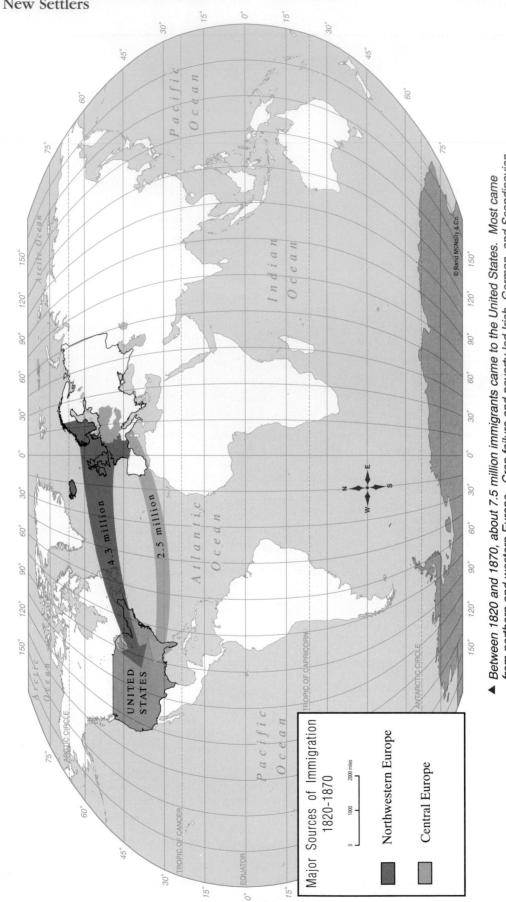

Major Sources of Immigration
1820-1870

Northwestern Europe

Central Europe

UNITED
STATES

4.3 million

2.5 million

▲ Between 1820 and 1870, about 7.5 million immigrants came to the United States. Most came from northern and western Europe. Crop failure and poverty led Irish, German, and Scandinavian immigrants to seek a better life in America.

Section 5   (1850-1865)

A Nation Divided

Between 1850 and 1860, differences between the North and the South widened. The agricultural economy of the South was based on slave labor. Many Northerners viewed slavery as wrong. **Abolitionists**, or people who demanded an end to slavery, operated the Underground Railroad to help slaves escape. The Compromise of 1850 and the Kansas-Nebraska Act attempted to settle the issue of slavery in the West.

When Abraham Lincoln was elected president in 1860, Southerners feared he would end slavery. Eleven southern states **seceded**, or withdrew, from the Union and formed the Confederacy. An attack on Fort Sumter in April 1861 marked the beginning of the Civil War. The war ended when Confederate general Robert E. Lee surrendered at Appomattox in April 1865.

The bitter war between the North and the South left lasting problems. Much of the South was destroyed. More Americans lost their lives in the Civil War than in any other war in which the United States has fought.

◀ *The Battle of Gettysburg took place at this site in Pennsylvania in July 1863.*

◀ *This memorial to Confederate leaders is carved on Stone Mountain near Atlanta, Georgia.*

Did You Know?

When Virginia seceded from the Union in 1861, 50 of its western counties separated from the state. These counties were admitted to the Union in 1863 as the state of West Virginia.

American Deaths in Major Wars

Civil War 618,000

World War II 405,000

Korean War 54,000

Vietnam War 58,000

Mexican War 13,000

World War I 117,000

	1850	1863	1865
People	Harriet Tubman leads slaves from Maryland to freedom in the North.	Abraham Lincoln delivers Gettysburg Address on battlefield in Pennsylvania.	Robert E. Lee surrenders at Appomattox Court House, Virginia.

	1860	1861	1865
Events	South Carolina becomes first southern state to secede.	Civil War begins at Fort Sumter, South Carolina.	Thirteenth Amendment ends slavery in the United States.

	1850	1852	1865
Literature	*The Scarlet Letter*, by Nathaniel Hawthorne, is set in Puritan New England.	*Uncle Tom's Cabin*, by Harriet Beecher Stowe, highlights the cruelty of slavery in the South.	"Drum Taps," by Walt Whitman, describes scenes from Civil War battlefields.

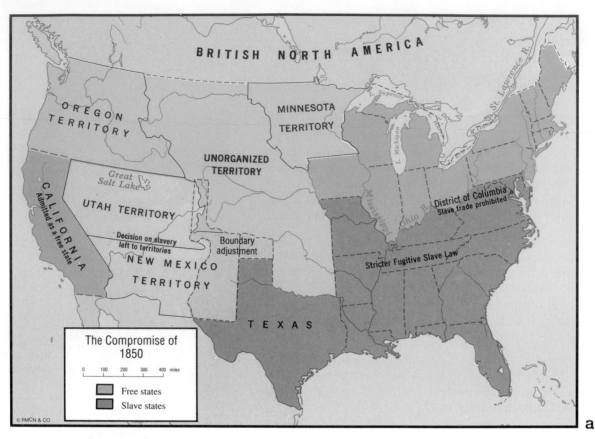

The Compromise of 1850

0 100 200 300 400 miles

Free states

Slave states

© RMCN & CO.

▲ *The Compromise of 1850 admitted California as a free state and ended slave trade in the District of Columbia. Utah and New Mexico Territories could decide the issue of slavery.*

Kansas–Nebraska Act, 1854

0 100 200 300 miles

© RMCN & CO.

▲ *The Kansas-Nebraska Act allowed settlers in those territories to decide whether to allow slavery.*

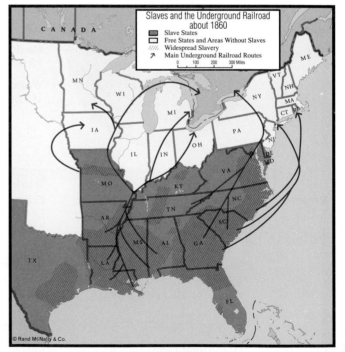

Slaves and the Underground Railroad about 1860

Slave States

Free States and Areas Without Slaves

Widespread Slavery

Main Underground Railroad Routes

0 100 200 300 Miles

© Rand McNally & Co.

▲ *The Underground Railroad was a system of escape routes slaves followed to freedom.*

41

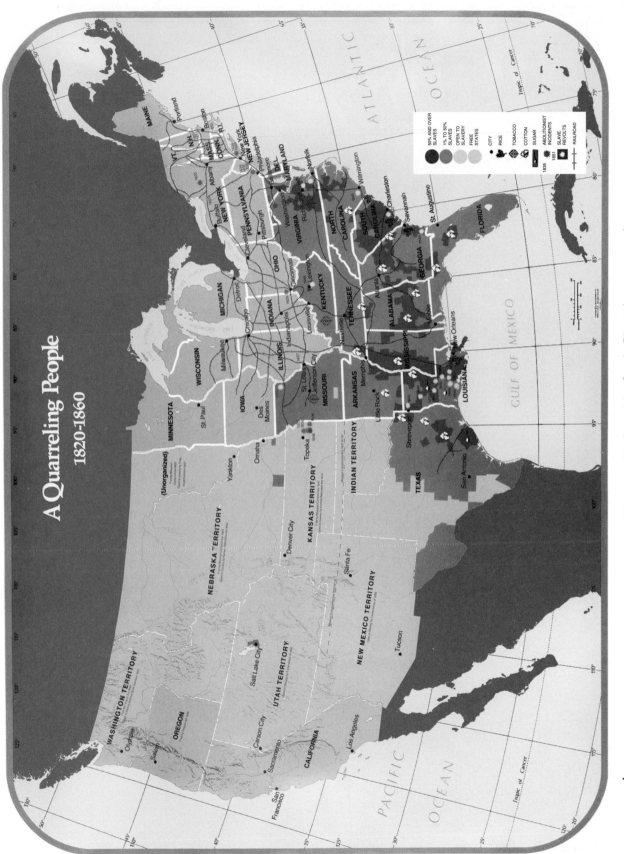

▲ Economic differences created different ways of life in the North and the South. Plantation crops, such as tobacco, cotton, and sugar cane, supported an agricultural economy based on slavery in the South. Advances in mass production and transportation supported an economy based on industry and trade in the North. Northern abolitionists viewed slavery as wrong and began a movement to end it.

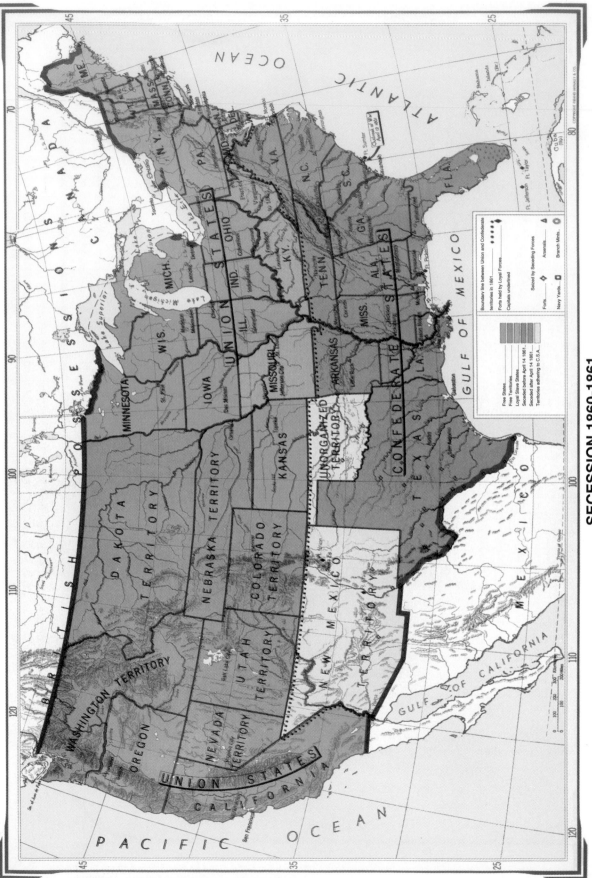

SECESSION 1860-1861

▲ The Confederate States of America consisted of eleven slave states that seceded from the Union in 1860 and 1861. The 23 remaining states and territories, including four slave states, fought for the Union during the Civil War.

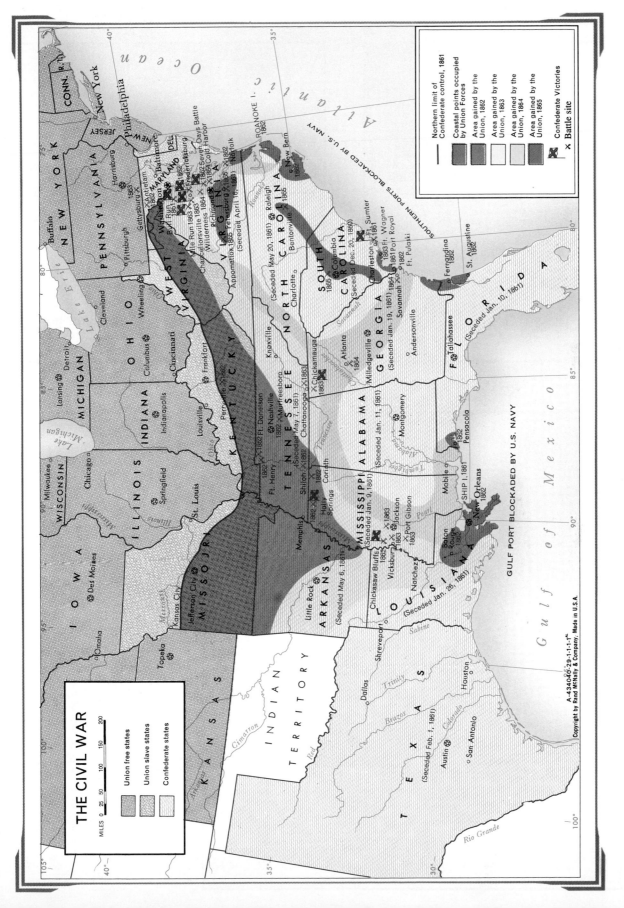

▲ *Most of the fighting in the East took place in Virginia. Much of the fighting in the West took place in Tennessee and along the Mississippi River. The map legend indicates how Union strategy succeeded by dividing the Confederacy and blockading its ports.*

THE CIVIL WAR

MILES 0 25 50 100 150 200

- Union free states
- Union slave states
- Confederate states

Northern limit of Confederate control, 1861
Coastal points occupied by Union Forces
Area gained by the Union, 1862
Area gained by the Union, 1863
Area gained by the Union, 1864
Area gained by the Union, 1865
X Confederate Victories
x Battle site

A-43406-29-1-1-1
Copyright by Rand McNally & Company. Made in U.S.A.

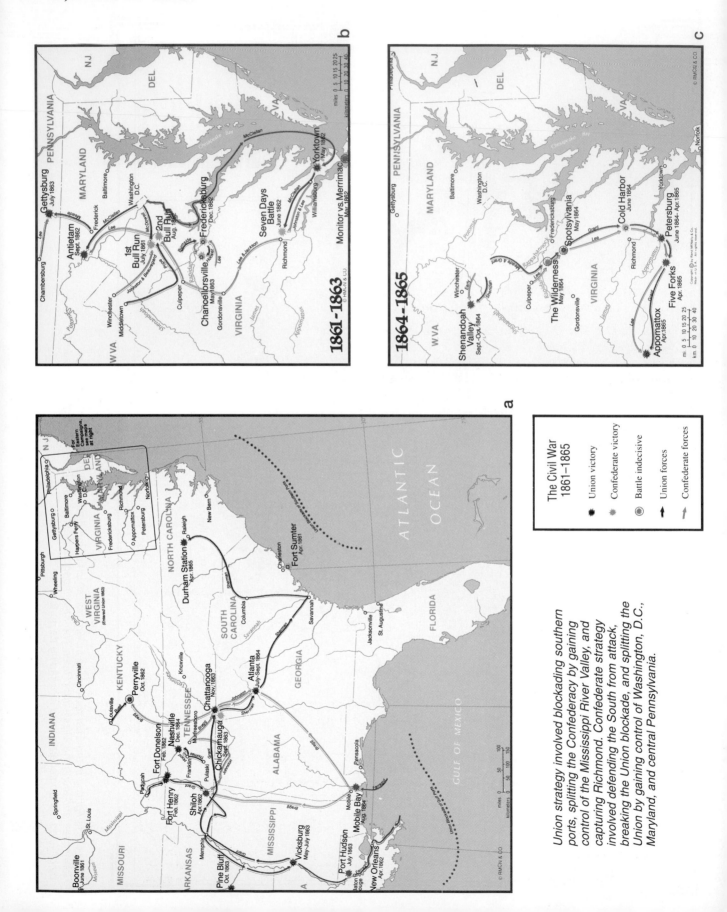

Union strategy involved blockading southern ports, splitting the Confederacy by gaining control of the Mississippi River Valley, and capturing Richmond. Confederate strategy involved defending the South from attack, breaking the Union blockade, and splitting the Union by gaining control of Washington, D.C., Maryland, and central Pennsylvania.

Section 6   *(1860-1920)*

Emerging as a Modern Nation

The years between 1860 and 1920 included the end of one era in American history and the beginning of another. The Great Plains opened to settlers as the U.S. Army defeated the Plains Indians and forced them onto reservations. Texas cattle ranchers drove their herds to railroads, which provided transportation to eastern markets. **Homesteaders**, or settlers who received free land from the government in exchange for farming it, moved to western territories. By 1890, the long process of settling the United States from coast to coast was complete. The American frontier had come to an end.

In the late 1800s, the United States began to emerge as a modern nation. Millions of immigrants came from Europe to farm the land or work in factories. The United States became an industrial nation and acquired territories overseas. It purchased Alaska and established naval bases on islands in the Pacific. It fought a war with Spain by which it acquired additional territories. The United States entered World War I in 1917 and assumed its role as a world power.

◀ *This statue of Buffalo Bill Cody in Wyoming represents the Old West.*

The Statue of Liberty ▶ *in New York Harbor has welcomed immigrants since 1886. It was a gift to the United States from France.*

Immigration to the United States, 1860-1919

Period	Millions of immigrants
1860-1869	~2
1870-1879	~2.7
1880-1889	~5
1890-1899	~4
1900-1909	~8
1910-1919	~6

Millions of immigrants (0, 2, 4, 6, 8)

Did You Know?

In 1850 about 20 million bison, or buffaloes, roamed the Great Plains. The westward movement almost wiped out these animals. By 1890, only about 500 bison could be found in the West.

	1877	**1889**	**1898**
People	Chief Joseph leads Nez Percés on a retreat through Idaho and Montana.	Jane Addams opens Hull House to help immigrants in Chicago.	Theodore Roosevelt leads Rough Riders in Cuba during Spanish-American War.
	1867	**1892**	**1898**
Events	United States purchases Alaska from Russia.	Ellis Island, in New York Harbor, becomes an immigration station.	Hawaii becomes a U.S. territory.
	1876	**1881**	**1912**
Literature	*The Adventures of Tom Sawyer,* by Mark Twain, is set in Hannibal, Missouri.	*A Century of Dishonor,* by Helen Hunt Jackson, describes mistreatment of Native Americans in the U.S.	*Riders of the Purple Sage,* by Zane Grey, describes life in the West.

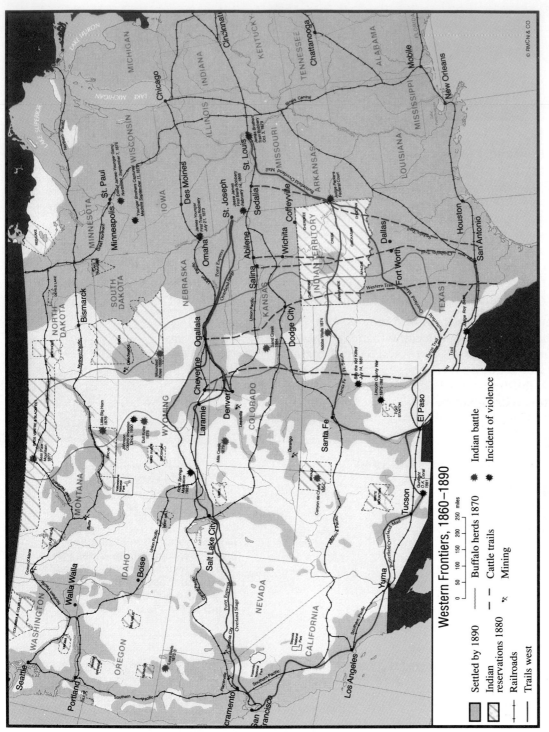

Western Frontiers, 1860–1890

0 50 100 150 200 250 miles

Settled by 1890 — **Buffalo herds 1870** ✳ **Indian battle**

Indian reservations 1880 – – **Cattle trails** ✳ **Incident of violence**

Railroads ✕ **Mining**

Trails west

© RMCN & CO

▲ *After 1860, the population west of the Mississippi River grew rapidly. Native Americans lost the battle to keep their lands, and the government moved them to reservations. Ranchers and farmers spread settlements throughout the Great Plains and the Far West. Although large areas of the West remained thinly populated, in 1890 the Census Bureau declared the frontier had come to an end.*

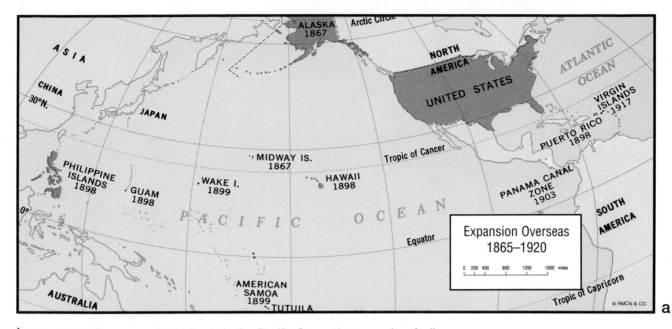

▲ The United States acquired islands in the Pacific Ocean that served as fueling stations for ships traveling to and from China and Japan. The Hawaiian Islands also provided raw materials for import or trade.

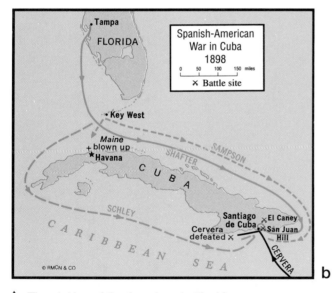

▲ The sinking of the American battleship Maine in Havana harbor brought the United States into war with Spain. The war was fought in both Cuba and the Philippines. As a result of the Spanish-American War, Spain granted freedom to Cuba and ceded Guam, Puerto Rico, and the Philippines to the United States.

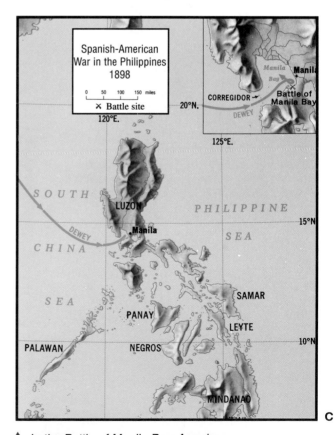

▲ In the Battle of Manila Bay, American ships commanded by Commodore George Dewey destroyed the Spanish fleet in the Philippines.

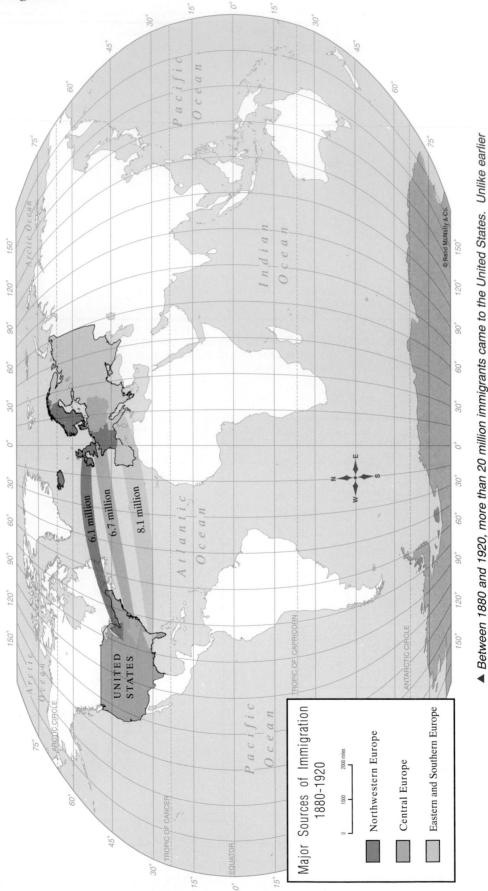

Major Sources of Immigration 1880–1920

- Northwestern Europe
- Central Europe
- Eastern and Southern Europe

▲ Between 1880 and 1920, more than 20 million immigrants came to the United States. Unlike earlier newcomers, who came mostly from northern and western Europe, these so-called "new immigrants" came mostly from central, eastern, and southern Europe.

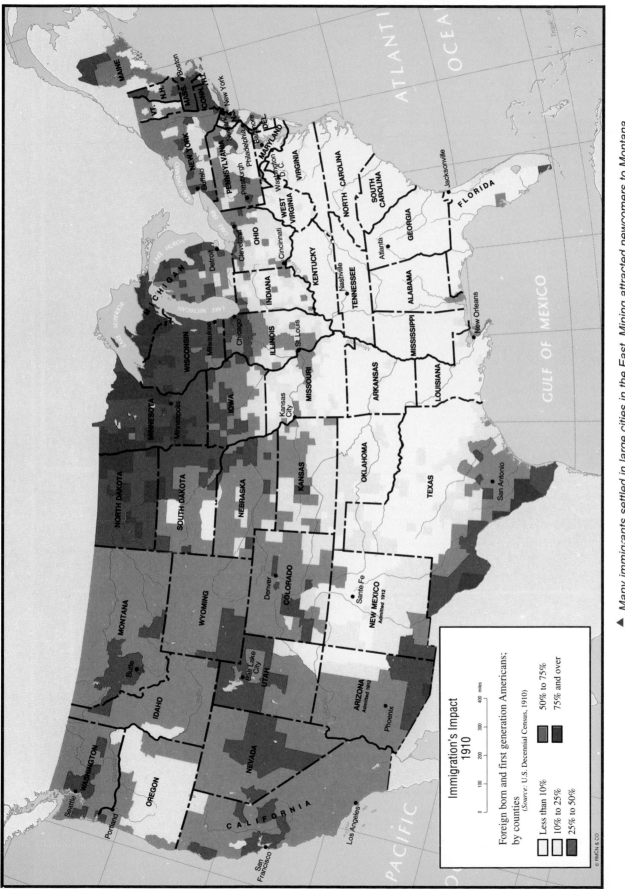

▲ *Many immigrants settled in large cities in the East. Mining attracted newcomers to Montana, Colorado, and Nevada. Railroad companies encouraged European workers to settle in the West. Poor economic conditions in Mexico led thousands of immigrants to settle in the United States.*

Immigration's Impact 1910

Foreign born and first generation Americans; by counties
(Source: U.S. Decennial Census, 1910)

- Less than 10%
- 10% to 25%
- 25% to 50%
- 50% to 75%
- 75% and over

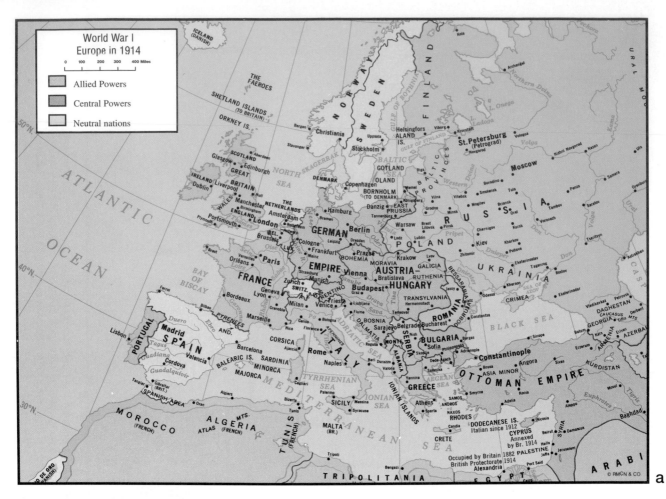

▲ In 1914, long-standing problems in Europe erupted in war between the Allied Powers and the Central Powers. The conflict, which became known as World War I, lasted four years. It involved more countries and caused more destruction than had any previous war.

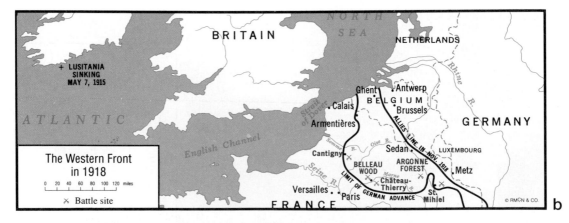

▲ The loss of American lives aboard the Lusitania helped draw the United States into the war in Europe. American troops helped the Allies defeat the Germans on the Western Front, which stretched through Belgium and France.

Section 7 *(1920-1999)*

Challenges & Changes in the 20th Century

During the decades between 1920 and 1999, the United States faced many challenges and experienced many changes. The economic prosperity of the 1920s ended with the stock market crash in 1929. Poverty and unemployment were widespread during the Great Depression of the 1930s. During World War II (1941-1945), United States troops fought in Europe and in the Pacific. After this war, the United States and the Soviet Union emerged as the world's leading powers.

The struggle between the Communist world, led by the Soviet Union, and the Democratic/Capitalist world, led by the United States, was called the **Cold War**. Between 1950 and 1990, the United States intervened in Korea, in Southeast Asia, and in Central America and the Caribbean to stop the spread of communism. The Cold War ended in 1991 when the Soviet Union was dissolved.

Changes took place within the United States as Americans moved from one area of the country to another, and suburbs grew around major cities. The **gross domestic product** (GDP), or value of all goods and services produced within the country, rose dramatically from the 1940s into the 1990s.

◀ *The United States Marine Corps Memorial in Arlington, Virginia, honors the flag raising on Iwo Jima during World War II.*

◀ *In 1940 Houston, Texas, ranked 21st in population among U.S. cities. By 1999, it was the nation's tenth largest metropolitan area.*

Gross Domestic Product, 1920-1999

Billions of dollars *(Current dollars)*

10,000 / 7,500 / 5,000 / 2,500 / 0

1920 1930 1940 1950 1960 1970 1980 1990 1999

Did You Know ?

Between 1941 and 1945, one in every five Americans moved from one part of the United States to another.

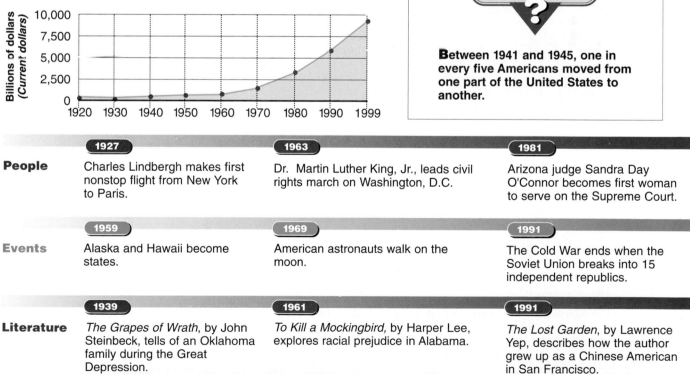

	People		
	1927 Charles Lindbergh makes first nonstop flight from New York to Paris.	**1963** Dr. Martin Luther King, Jr., leads civil rights march on Washington, D.C.	**1981** Arizona judge Sandra Day O'Connor becomes first woman to serve on the Supreme Court.
Events	**1959** Alaska and Hawaii become states.	**1969** American astronauts walk on the moon.	**1991** The Cold War ends when the Soviet Union breaks into 15 independent republics.
Literature	**1939** *The Grapes of Wrath*, by John Steinbeck, tells of an Oklahoma family during the Great Depression.	**1961** *To Kill a Mockingbird*, by Harper Lee, explores racial prejudice in Alabama.	**1991** *The Lost Garden*, by Lawrence Yep, describes how the author grew up as a Chinese American in San Francisco.

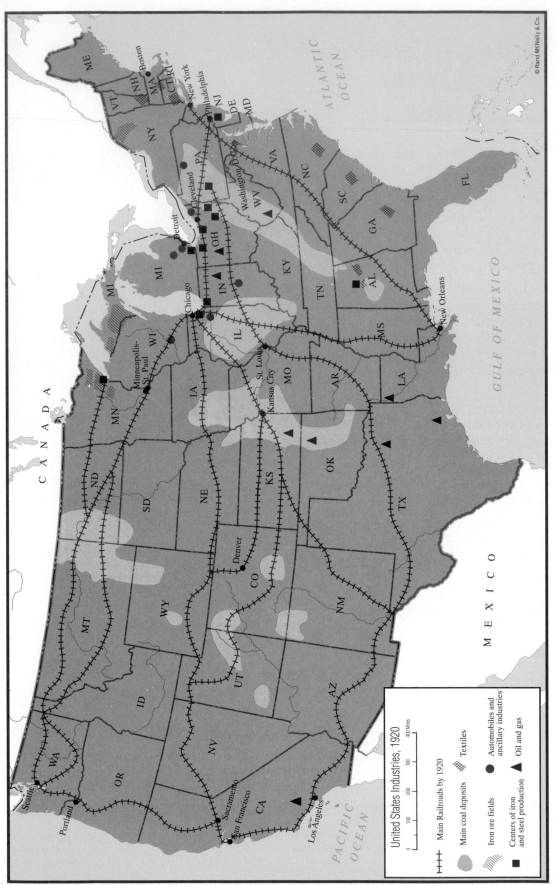

▲ By 1920 the United States was a leading industrial nation. Advances in technology enabled workers to produce more goods faster. The demand for petroleum and steel increased to meet the growing needs of new industries such as the automobile industry. Spectacular economic growth provided a high standard of living for many Americans.

© Rand McNally & Co.

United States Industries, 1920

┼┼┼	Main Railroads by 1920
(shaded)	Main coal deposits
(hatched)	Iron ore fields
■	Centers of iron and steel production
▨	Textiles
●	Automobiles and ancillary industries
▲	Oil and gas

0   100   200   300   400 Miles

53

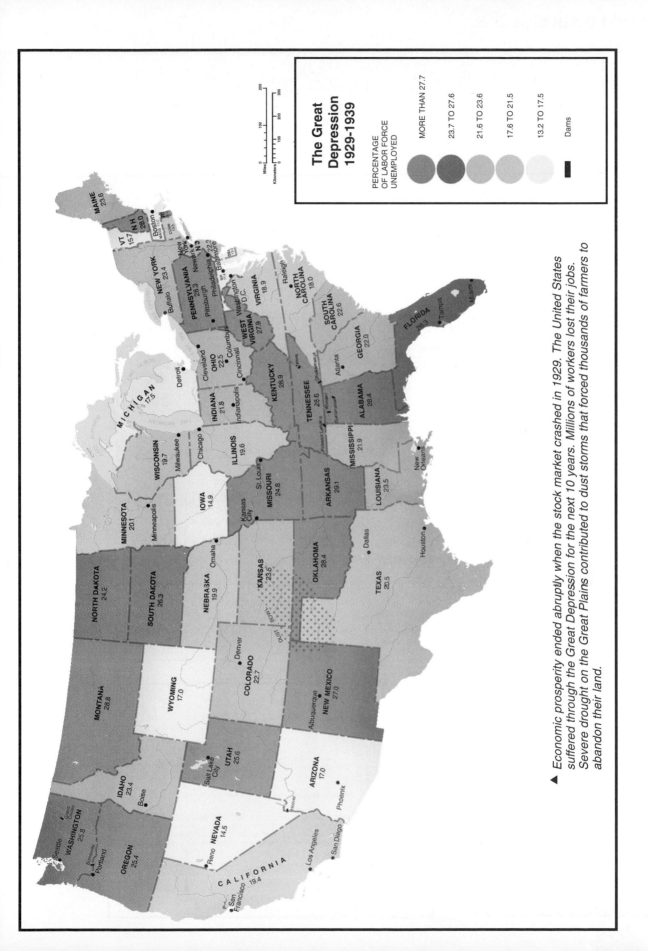

▲ Economic prosperity ended abruptly when the stock market crashed in 1929. The United States suffered through the Great Depression for the next 10 years. Millions of workers lost their jobs. Severe drought on the Great Plains contributed to dust storms that forced thousands of farmers to abandon their land.

The Great Depression 1929-1939

PERCENTAGE OF LABOR FORCE UNEMPLOYED

MORE THAN 27.7
23.7 TO 27.6
21.6 TO 23.6
17.6 TO 21.5
13.2 TO 17.5
Dams

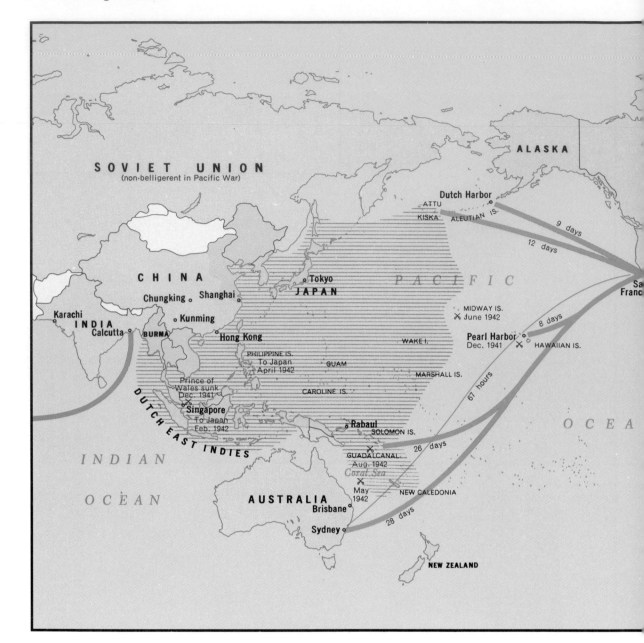

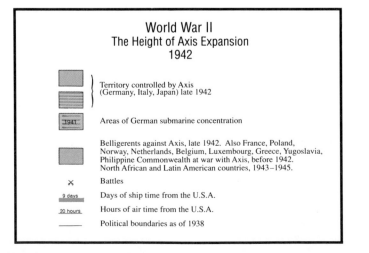

World War II
The Height of Axis Expansion
1942

Territory controlled by Axis
(Germany, Italy, Japan) late 1942

1941 Areas of German submarine concentration

Belligerents against Axis, late 1942. Also France, Poland,
Norway, Netherlands, Belgium, Luxembourg, Greece, Yugoslavia,
Philippine Commonwealth at war with Axis, before 1942.
North African and Latin American countries, 1943–1945.

× Battles

9 days Days of ship time from the U.S.A.

20 hours Hours of air time from the U.S.A.

——— Political boundaries as of 1938

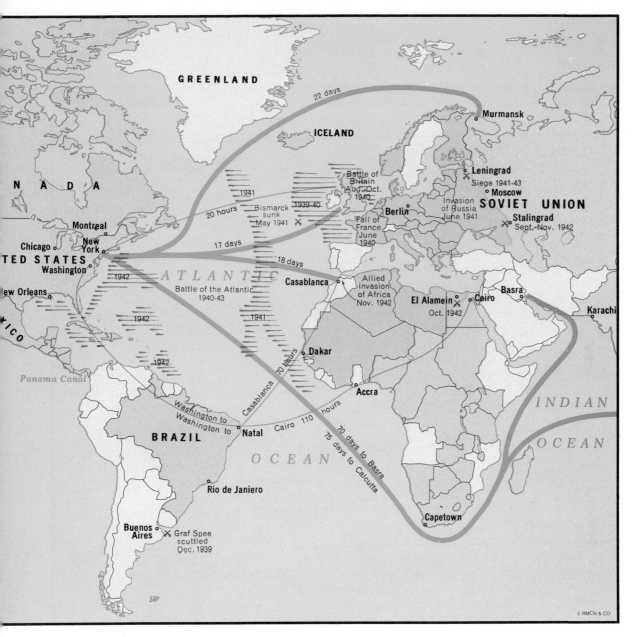

The following labels appear on the map:

GREENLAND

ICELAND

22 days

Murmansk

Battle of Britain Aug.-Oct. 1940

Leningrad
Siege 1941-43

NADA

1941

20 hours

Bismarck sunk May 1941

1939-40

Fall of France June 1940

Moscow

SOVIET UNION

Invasion of Russia June 1941

Stalingrad Sept.-Nov. 1942

Montreal

New York

17 days

18 days

Berlin

Chicago

TED STATES

Washington

Casablanca

Allied invasion of Africa Nov. 1942

El Alamein Oct. 1942

Cairo

Basra

ew Orleans

1942

ATLANTIC

Battle of the Atlantic 1940-43

Karachi

ICO

1942

1941

Dakar

Panama Canal

1942

70 hours

Accra

INDIAN

Washington to Casablanca 70 hours

Washington to Cairo 110 hours

70 days to Basra

75 days to Calcutta

OCEAN

BRAZIL

Natal

OCEAN

Rio de Janiero

Capetown

Buenos Aires

Graf Spee scuttled Dec. 1939

© RMCN & CO.

▲ World War II began in 1939 when Germany, under Nazi dictator Adolf Hitler,
invaded Poland. The Axis powers (Germany, Italy, Japan, and their partners)
fought against the Allied powers (shown in gold on the map). Few nations
remained neutral. By 1942 the Axis controlled most of Europe, northern Africa,
and parts of Asia and the Pacific. German submarines attacked Allied cargo
ships in the Atlantic.

The Japanese attack on Pearl Harbor, Hawaii, in December 1941 brought the
United States into the war. American troops and supplies were sent to Europe
and to the Pacific. The map indicates transportation time by air and by water
from the United States to selected sites. During 1942, Allied forces halted Axis
expansion in northern Africa, the Soviet Union, and the Pacific.

ALASKA

SOVIET UNION

Kiska & Attu
June 1942

MONGOLIA

MANCHURIA

Peking

KOREA

JAPAN

Tokyo

CHINA

Shanghai

Hiroshima
Aug. 1945

Midway Island
June 1942

Chungking

Hwang Ho

Yangtze

Okinawa
Mar.-Apr. 1945

Iwo Jima
Feb. 1945

Wake Island
Dec. 1941

INDIA

Hong Kong

BURMA

FRENCH
INDOCHINA

Mekong

Philippine Sea
June 1944

Saipan, Tinian, & Guam
June-July 1944

THAILAND

PHILIPPINES

Bataan
Jan.-Feb. 1942

Leyte Gulf
Oct. 1944

Eniwetok
Feb. 1944

MALAYA

BRUNEI N BORNEO

SARAWAK

Truk Islands
Feb. 1944

Kwajalein
Jan. 1944

SUMATRA

Singapore

BORNEO

Hollandia
Apr. 1944

Bougainville
Nov. 1943

Tarawa
Nov. 1943

PACIFIC
OCEAN

NEW GUINEA

Empress Augusta Bay
Nov. 1943

Guadalcanal
Aug. 1942-Feb. 1943

INDIAN
OCEAN

Coral Sea
May 1942

Equator

AUSTRALIA

miles 0   250   500   750   1000
kilometers 0   500   1000   1500

World War II
1941–1945
Pacific Theater

Allied powers

Axis powers   Battles

Axis controlled ⬅ Allied advances
areas

▲ In 1943 and 1944, the Allies captured
Japanese-held islands in the Pacific. In
August 1945, the United States dropped
an atomic bomb on Hiroshima, Japan.
World War II ended when the Japanese
surrendered in September 1945.

▲ After defeating the Axis in northern Africa, the Allies focused on Europe. Italy surrendered in 1943. In 1944 Allies landed in northern France and advanced on Germany from the west, while Soviet troops advanced from the east. Germany surrendered in May 1945.

World War II
1941–1945
European Theater

Allied powers   Neutral nations

Axis powers   Battles

Axis controlled areas   Allied advances

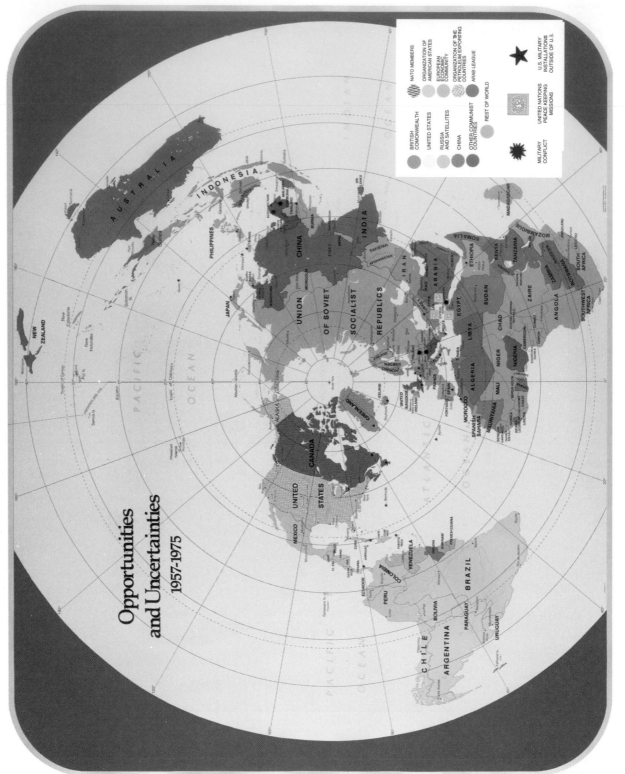

▲ In 1949 the United States and other free nations formed a military alliance called the North Atlantic Treaty Organization (NATO) to prevent the spread of communism. The Soviet Union and other communist countries formed a competing alliance called the Warsaw Pact. This view indicates why Canada and the United States feared a possible Soviet attack from the north.

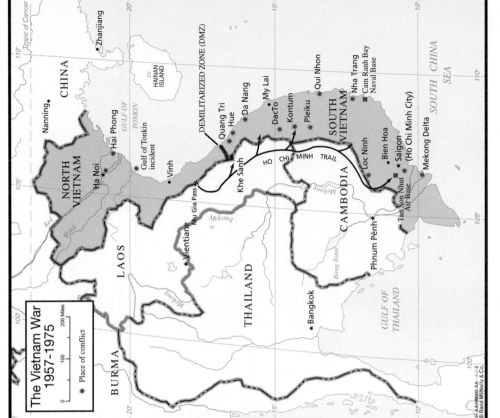

b

The Vietnam War 1957–1975

Scale:
0 100 200 Miles

✱ Place of conflict

H-AAH6000-AB- -1-2-2
© Rand McNally & Co.

▲ The United States entered the longest war in its history to prevent communist-ruled North Vietnam from taking over non-communist South Vietnam. The Ho Chi Minh Trail was a system of roads the North Vietnamese used as a supply route for the Viet Cong, or communist rebels in South Vietnam.

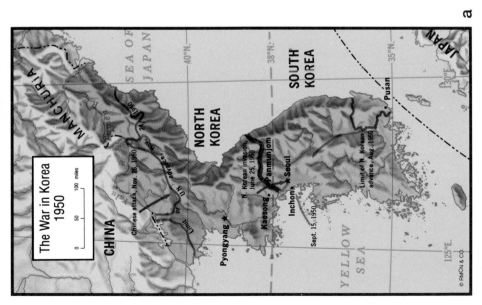

a

The War in Korea 1950

Scale:
0 50 100 miles

© RMCN & CO

▲ United Nations members, including the United States, sent troops to defend South Korea from an invasion by communist-ruled North Korea. In 1950, UN forces halted the North Korean advance at Pusan and pushed to the Yalu River in the north. The war ended in 1953 when the UN and North Korea signed an armistice agreement.

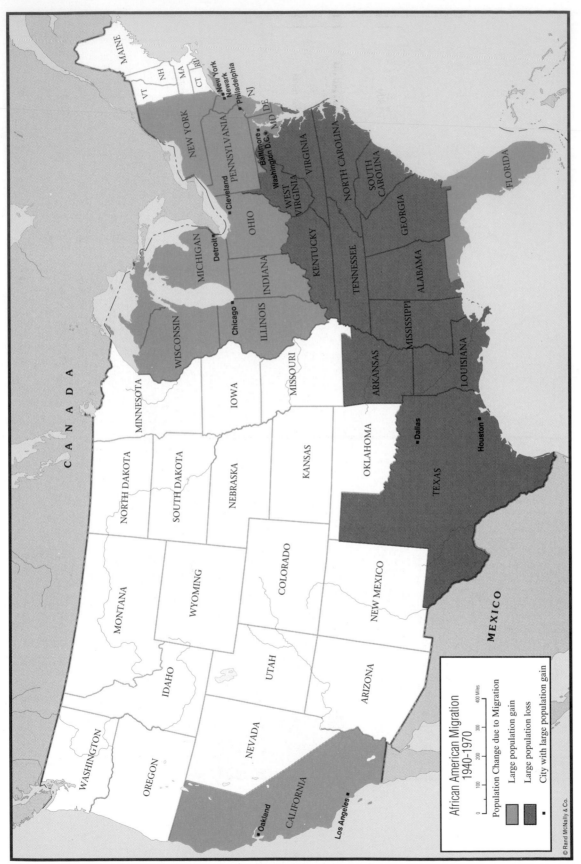

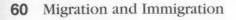

▲ *Between 1940 and 1970, millions of African Americans moved out of the South. More than two-thirds of the total African American population relocated to cities. More than half the urban black population was concentrated in the twelve cities shown on the map.*

African American Migration 1940-1970

Population Change due to Migration

Large population gain

Large population loss

■ City with large population gain

0   100   200   300   400 Miles

© Rand McNally & Co.

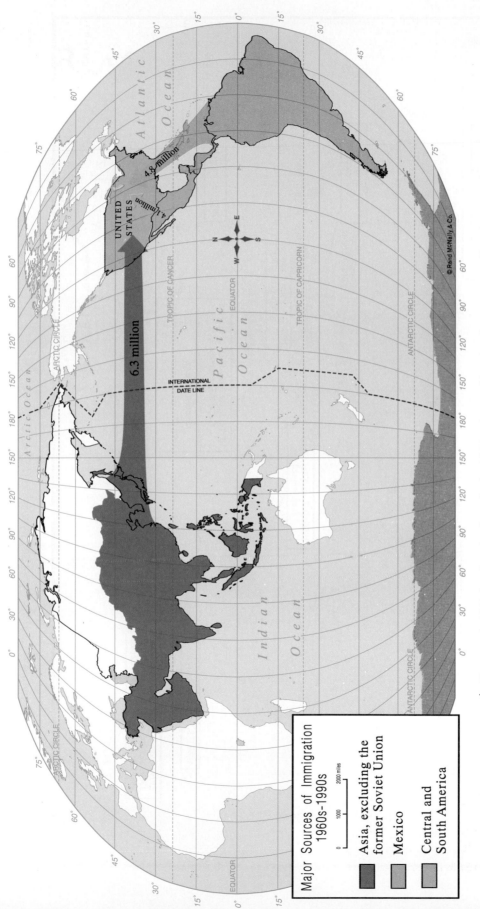

Major Sources of Immigration 1960s–1990s

- Asia, excluding the former Soviet Union
- Mexico
- Central and South America

0   1000   2000 miles

UNITED STATES

4.8 million

4.1 million

6.3 million

INTERNATIONAL DATE LINE

N E S W

©Rand McNally & Co.

Atlantic Ocean

Pacific Ocean

Arctic Ocean

Indian Ocean

TROPIC OF CANCER

EQUATOR

TROPIC OF CAPRICORN

ANTARCTIC CIRCLE

ARCTIC CIRCLE

▲ *Changes in U.S. immigration laws in the 1960s changed immigration patterns. Percentages of immigrants from Europe decreased. In the 1990s, most immigrants to the United States came from Mexico, the Philippines, Haiti, China, India, Vietnam, Jamaica, Cuba, and South Korea.*

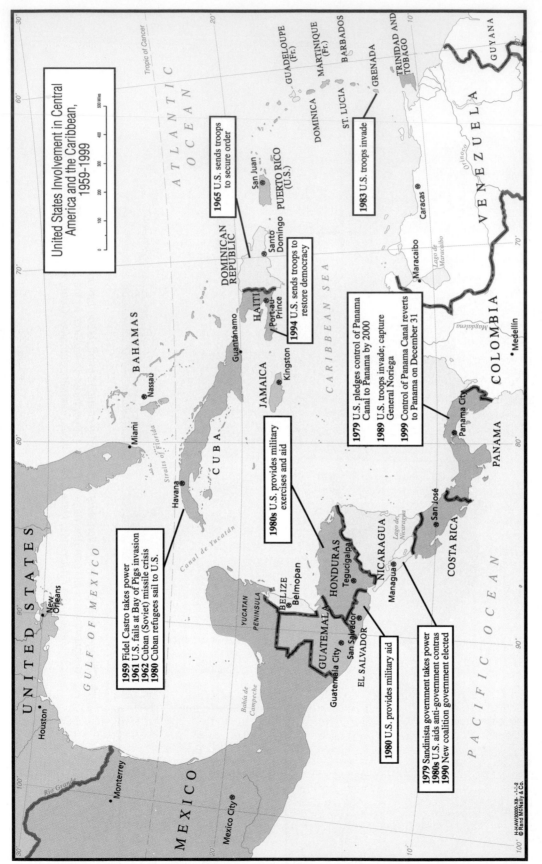

United States Involvement in Central America and the Caribbean, 1959-1999

1965 U.S. sends troops to secure order

1983 U.S. troops invade

1994 U.S. sends troops to restore democracy

1979 U.S. pledges control of Panama Canal to Panama by 2000
1989 U.S. troops invade; capture General Noriega
1999 Control of Panama Canal reverts to Panama on December 31

1980s U.S. provides military exercises and aid

1959 Fidel Castro takes power
1961 U.S. fails at Bay of Pigs invasion
1962 Cuban (Soviet) missile crisis
1980 Cuban refugees sail to U.S.

1980 U.S. provides military aid

1979 Sandinista government takes power
1980s U.S. aids anti-government contras
1990 New coalition government elected

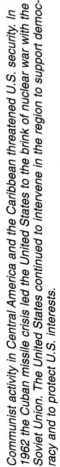

▲ *Communist activity in Central America and the Caribbean threatened U.S. security. In 1962 the Cuban missile crisis led the United States to the brink of nuclear war with the Soviet Union. The United States continued to intervene in the region to support democracy and to protect U.S. interests.*

Section 8   *(2000 & beyond)*

Entering a New Millennium

In 2000 the United States was one of the world's leading nations. Its resources and technology made it a leader in the production of goods and services. Its principles of freedom and opportunity provided its people with one of the world's highest standards of living. The advent of the Internet had made it easy to exchange ideas and information quickly.

The diverse population of the United States reflected the history of a nation settled by people from every part of the world. According to the 2000 census, most Americans throughout the country lived in large **metropolitan areas**, or cities surrounded by suburbs. They earned more money and lived longer than Americans in the past. In spite of widespread prosperity, however, many Americans lived in poverty.

As the United States entered a new millennium, it faced new challenges in a changing world. Americans showed courage and resolve in response to terrorist attacks on New York City and Washington, D.C. on September 11, 2001. Defending human rights, supporting economic development, and protecting the environment have become global issues.

◄ *Skyscrapers tower over midtown Manhattan in New York – the largest U.S. city in population in 2000. Plans have been made for new buildings and a memorial park to replace the World Trade Center towers.*

Seattle, Washington, became an aerospace and technology center as well as a leading U.S. port for Pacific Rim trade. ▶

Did You Know ?

The Los Angeles metropolitan area has the largest concentration of immigrants in the country. Nearly one-third of its residents moved there from other countries.

Population Distribution by Age, 1900 and 2000

Age groups: 0-4, 5-14, 15-24, 25-34, 35-44, 45-54, 55-64, 65+

Percent of population: 5, 10, 15, 20, 25

	2001	2002	2002
People	Condeleeza Rice becomes the first woman and the first African American to be named National Security Advisor.	Ellen Ochoa, co-inventor of optical analysis systems and the first Hispanic female astronaut, makes her fourth voyage on the space shuttle.	Former president Jimmy Carter receives the Nobel Peace Price for his work in finding solutions to international conflicts.
	2001	**2003**	**2004**
Events	Terrorists attack the World Trade center and the Pentagon on September 11. In response, U.S.-led forces attack Afghanistan.	Scientists finish mapping the entire human genome, which contains the complete genetic formula for a human being.	School children log onto the Internet to view images sent from the surface of Mars by two U.S.-launched robotized rovers.
	2000	**2001**	**2002**
Literature	*Interpreter of Maladies*, by Jhumpa Lahiri, wins a Pulitzer Prize for its stories about immigrants from India who come to the United States.	*Pleasure Dome*, a collection of poems by Yusef Komunyakaa, explores such topics as his Southern roots, his experiences in Vietnam, and jazz music.	*A Song Flung Up to Heaven*, by Maya Angelou, completes the autobiography of the African American poet.

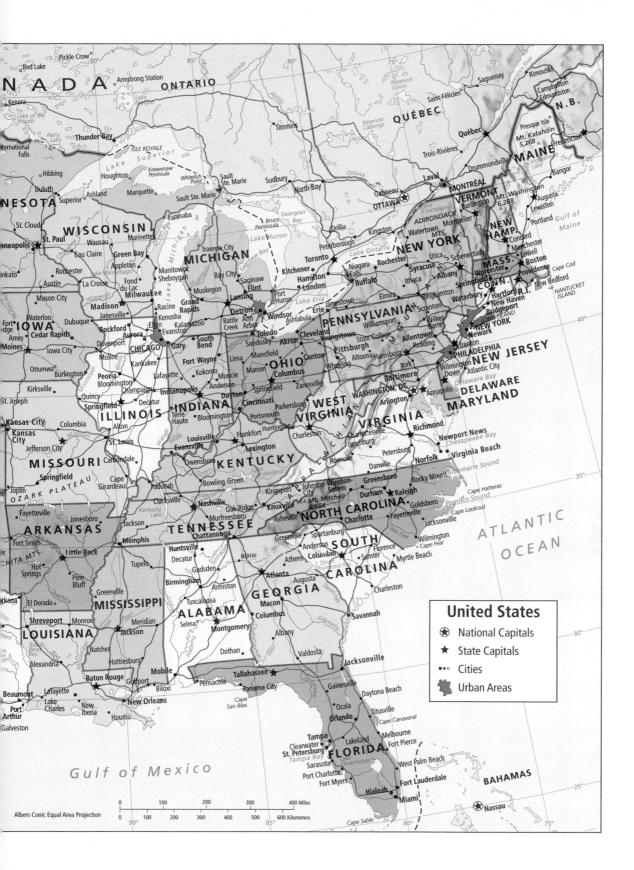

CANADA · Pickle Crow · Red Lake · Armstrong Station · ONTARIO · Kenora · Lake of the Woods · Rainy Lake · International Falls · Hibbing · Duluth · MINNESOTA · St. Cloud · Minneapolis · St. Paul · Mankato · Rochester · Austin · Mason City · Fort Dodge · Waterloo · Ames · Des Moines · Iowa City · IOWA · Cedar Rapids · Dubuque · Davenport · Moline · Burlington · Ottumwa · St. Joseph · Kirksville · Quincy · Springfield · Decatur · Kansas City · Columbia · Jefferson City · MISSOURI · Springfield · Joplin · OZARK PLATEAU · Fayetteville · Jonesboro · Fort Smith · ARKANSAS · Little Rock · Pine Bluff · Hot Springs · OUACHITA MTS. · El Dorado · Texarkana · Shreveport · Monroe · LOUISIANA · Alexandria · Natchez · Baton Rouge · Beaumont · Lafayette · Port Arthur · Lake Charles · New Iberia · Houma · New Orleans · Galveston

Armstrong Station · ONTARIO · Thunder Bay · Lake Superior · ISLE ROYALE · Keweenaw Peninsula · Houghton · Ashland · Marquette · Escanaba · Whitefish Point · Sault Ste. Marie · Sudbury · North Bay · Timmins · Missinaibi River · Abitibi River · Réservoir Gouin · QUÉBEC · Saguenay · Rimouski · Campbellton · Edmundston · N.B. · Saint-Félicien · Québec · Trois-Rivières · Drummondville · Fredericton · Presque Isle · Mt. Katahdin 5,268 · MAINE · Bangor · Moosehead Lake · WISCONSIN · Superior · Wausau · Eau Claire · Green Bay · Appleton · La Crosse · Fond du Lac · Manitowoc · Sheboygan · Marinette · Madison · Janesville · Milwaukee · Racine · Kenosha · Lake Winnebago · Lake Michigan · MICHIGAN · Traverse City · Bay City · Saginaw · Muskegon · Grand Rapids · Flint · Lansing · Battle Creek · Kalamazoo · Ann Arbor · Detroit · Windsor · Georgian Bay · Bruce Peninsula · Lake Huron · Saginaw Bay · Kitchener · Hamilton · London · Port Huron · Lake St. Clair · Orillia · Peterborough · Toronto · Lake Ontario · Kingston · Gatineau · OTTAWA · Ottawa River · Laval · MONTRÉAL · Burlington · VERMONT · Montpelier · Mt. Washington 6,288 · NEW HAMP. · Concord · Manchester · Lowell · Augusta · Lewiston · Portland · Gulf of Maine

ADIRONDACK MTS. · Watertown · NEW YORK · Rochester · Syracuse · Utica · Schenectady · Albany · Niagara Falls · Buffalo · Ithaca · Elmira · Binghamton · Scranton · Wilkes-Barre · MASS. · Springfield · Worcester · Boston · CONN. · Hartford · Providence · R.I. · New Bedford · Cape Cod · NANTUCKET ISLAND · Waterbury · New Haven · Bridgeport · LONG ISLAND · NEW YORK · Newark · Allentown · Reading · Trenton · NEW JERSEY · PENNSYLVANIA · Williamsport · State College · Altoona · Harrisburg · York · PHILADELPHIA · Wilmington · Dover · Atlantic City · Delaware Bay · DELAWARE · Erie · Ashtabula · Cleveland · Youngstown · Pittsburgh · Wheeling · Akron · Canton · OHIO · Columbus · Sandusky · Toledo · Mansfield · Zanesville · Baltimore · Annapolis · MARYLAND · WASHINGTON, D.C. · Arlington · WEST VIRGINIA · Parkersburg · Charleston · Huntington · VIRGINIA · Richmond · Charlottesville · Lynchburg · Petersburg · Newport News · Norfolk · Virginia Beach · Chesapeake Bay

Rockford · Aurora · Elgin · Evanston · CHICAGO · Gary · South Bend · Fort Wayne · Kankakee · Lafayette · Kokomo · Muncie · Anderson · INDIANA · Peoria · Bloomington · Champaign · ILLINOIS · Springfield · Decatur · Terre Haute · Bloomington · Indianapolis · Dayton · Cincinnati · Springfield · Lima · Marion · Alton · St. Louis · Carbondale · Cape Girardeau · Paducah · Clarksville · Nashville · Oak Ridge · Knoxville · Louisville · Frankfort · Lexington · Evansville · Owensboro · Bowling Green · KENTUCKY · Kingsport · Johnson City · Winston-Salem · Greensboro · Durham · Raleigh · Rocky Mount · Mt. Mitchell 6,684 · APPALACHIAN · Asheville · Charlotte · NORTH CAROLINA · Goldsboro · Fayetteville · Cape Hatteras · Pamlico Sound · Albemarle Sound · Roanoke · Danville · Charleston · Kentucky Lake

TENNESSEE · Memphis · Jackson · Huntsville · Decatur · Gadsden · Chattanooga · Rome · Athens · Spartanburg · Greenville · Anderson · Columbia · Sumter · SOUTH CAROLINA · Florence · Myrtle Beach · Cape Fear · Wilmington · Cape Lookout · Jacksonville · MISSISSIPPI · Tupelo · Birmingham · Anniston · Tuscaloosa · ALABAMA · Selma · Montgomery · GEORGIA · Columbus · Macon · Augusta · Savannah · Charleston · Greenville · Meridian · Jackson · Hattiesburg · Mobile · Gulfport · Biloxi · Pensacola · Panama City · Dothan · Albany · Valdosta · Tallahassee · Cape San Blas · ATLANTIC OCEAN

Gulf of Mexico · FLORIDA · Jacksonville · Gainesville · Ocala · Daytona Beach · Titusville · Orlando · Cape Canaveral · Tampa · Clearwater · St. Petersburg · Tampa Bay · Lakeland · Melbourne · Fort Pierce · Sarasota · Lake Okeechobee · West Palm Beach · Port Charlotte · Fort Myers · Fort Lauderdale · Hialeah · Miami · BAHAMAS · Nassau · Cape Sable

United States

⚹ National Capitals
★ State Capitals
•·• Cities
🗺 Urban Areas

Albers Conic Equal Area Projection

0   100   200   300   400 Miles
0 100 200 300 400 500 600 Kilometers

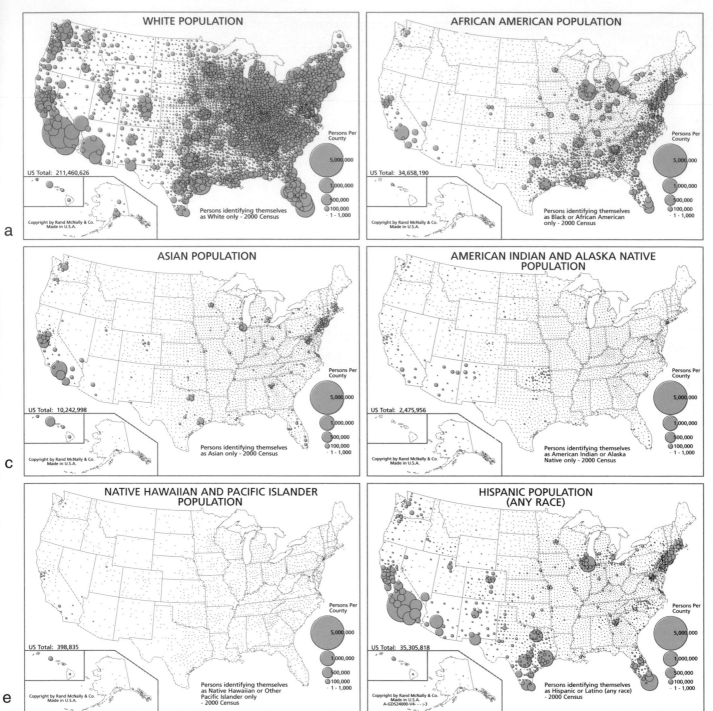

WHITE POPULATION

US Total: 211,460,626

Persons Per County

5,000,000
1,000,000
500,000
100,000
1 - 1,000

Persons identifying themselves as White only - 2000 Census

Copyright by Rand McNally & Co.
Made in U.S.A.

AFRICAN AMERICAN POPULATION

US Total: 34,658,190

Persons Per County

5,000,000
1,000,000
500,000
100,000
1 - 1,000

Persons identifying themselves as Black or African American only - 2000 Census

Copyright by Rand McNally & Co.
Made in U.S.A.

ASIAN POPULATION

US Total: 10,242,998

Persons Per County

5,000,000
1,000,000
500,000
100,000
1 - 1,000

Persons identifying themselves as Asian only - 2000 Census

Copyright by Rand McNally & Co.
Made in U.S.A.

AMERICAN INDIAN AND ALASKA NATIVE POPULATION

US Total: 2,475,956

Persons Per County

5,000,000
1,000,000
500,000
100,000
1 - 1,000

Persons identifying themselves as American Indian or Alaska Native only - 2000 Census

Copyright by Rand McNally & Co.
Made in U.S.A.

NATIVE HAWAIIAN AND PACIFIC ISLANDER POPULATION

US Total: 398,835

Persons Per County

5,000,000
1,000,000
500,000
100,000
1 - 1,000

Persons identifying themselves as Native Hawaiian or Other Pacific Islander only - 2000 Census

Copyright by Rand McNally & Co.
Made in U.S.A.

HISPANIC POPULATION (ANY RACE)

US Total: 35,305,818

Persons Per County

5,000,000
1,000,000
500,000
100,000
1 - 1,000

Persons identifying themselves as Hispanic or Latino (any race) - 2000 Census

Copyright by Rand McNally & Co.
Made in U.S.A.
A-GDS24000-V4- - 3-3

a

b

c

d

e

f

These maps show some major racial/ethnic groups in the United States in 2000 and where they lived.

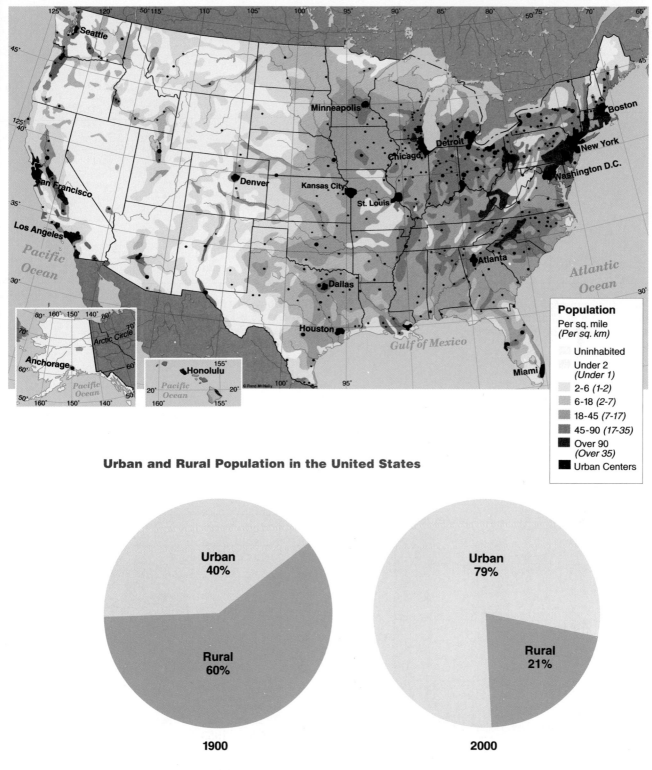

Urban and Rural Population in the United States

Population

Per sq. mile
(Per sq. km)

Uninhabited

Under 2
(Under 1)

2-6 *(1-2)*

6-18 *(2-7)*

18-45 *(7-17)*

45-90 *(17-35)*

Over 90
(Over 35)

Urban Centers

Urban
40%

Rural
60%

1900

Urban
79%

Rural
21%

2000

In 2000 more than three-fourths of all Americans lived in urban areas. The map shows the locations of the most densely populated parts of the United States. Notice that several metropolitan areas from Boston to Washington D.C. have grown together to form a large, densely populated area called a megalopolis. The circle graphs compare the percentages of urban and rural population in the United States in 1900 and 2000.

Median Family Income, 2000

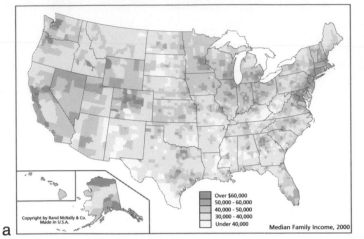

▲ The map shows median family income, or the middle value of all family incomes, in different parts of the United States in 2000.

High School Graduation, 2000

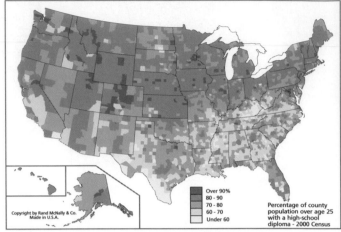

▲ The map shows the percent of people over age 25 who obtained a high school diploma in different parts of the United States in 2000.

Median Family Income (in current dollars), 1950-2000

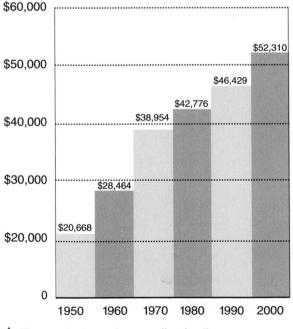

▲ The graph shows how median family income throughout the United States changed between 1950 and 2000.

High School Graduation Statistics 1940-2000

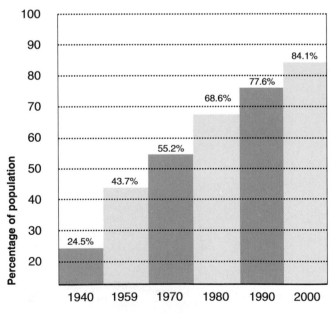

▲ The graph shows how the percentage of persons 25 years or older who obtained a high school diploma changed in the United States between 1940 and 2000.

Percentage of U.S. Population Below Poverty Level, 2000

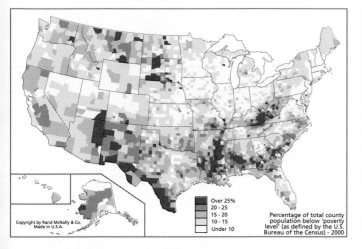

▲ The map shows the percentages of people living below the poverty level in different parts of the United States in 2000. Poverty level is based on the income needed to feed a family adequately without spending more than a third of the family income on food.

U.S. Unemployment Rates, 2000

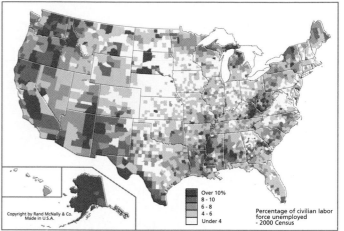

▲ The map shows the percentages of unemployed workers in different parts of the United States in 2000.

Percentage of U.S. Population Below Poverty Level, 1960-2000

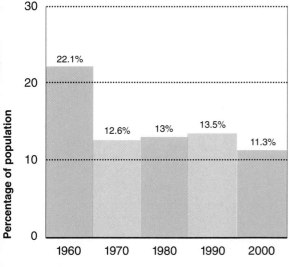

▲ The graph shows how the percentage of Americans below the poverty level changed between 1960 and 2000.

U.S. Unemployment Rates, 1960-2000

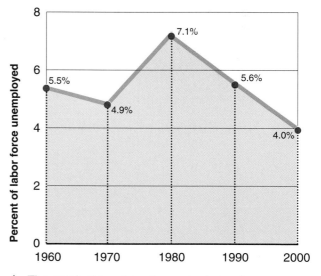

▲ The graph shows how the percentage of unemployed workers in the United States changed between 1960 and 2000.

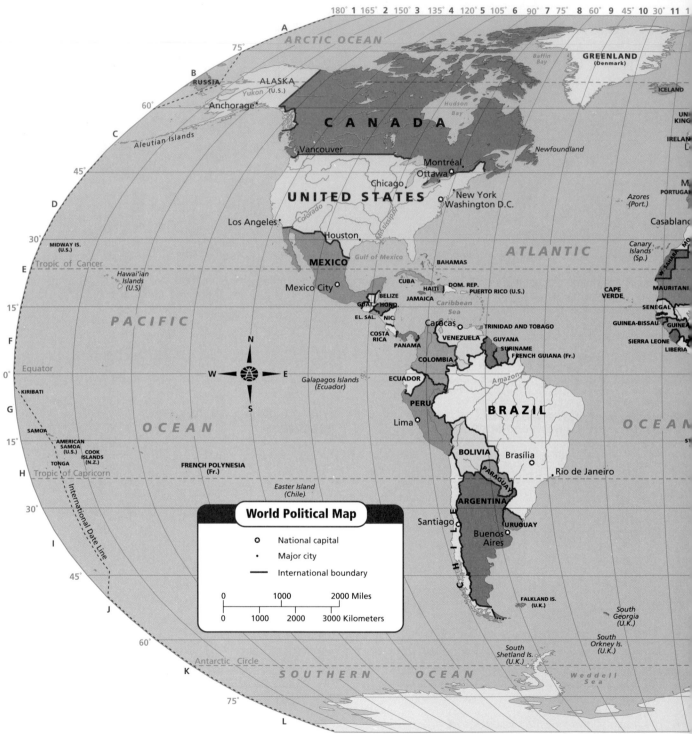

180° **1** 165° **2** 150° **3** 135° **4** 120° **5** 105° **6** 90° **7** 75° **8** 60° **9** 45° **10** 30° **11** 1

A ARCTIC OCEAN

75°

GREENLAND
(Denmark)

B RUSSIA ALASKA
(U.S.)
Yukon

Baffin
Bay

ICELAND

60° Anchorage

CANADA

Hudson
Bay

Newfoundland

UNI
KING

C Aleutian Islands

Vancouver

IRELAN

45° Montréal
Ottawa

Chicago

New York
Washington D.C.

D UNITED STATES

Colorado

Azores
(Port.)

PORTUGA

M

30° Los Angeles

Houston

Canary
Islands
(Sp.)

Casablanc

E MIDWAY IS.
(U.S.)
Tropic of Cancer

MEXICO

Mississippi

Gulf of Mexico

ATLANTIC

W. SAHARA

MO

BAHAMAS

MAURITANI

Hawai'ian
Islands
(U.S.)

Mexico City

CUBA

HAITI

DOM. REP.

PUERTO RICO (U.S.)

CAPE
VERDE

15° PACIFIC

JAMAICA

BELIZE
HOND.

GUAT.

Caribbean
Sea

SENEGAL

GUINEA-BISSAU

GUINEA

F EL. SAL.

COSTA
RICA

NIC.

Caracas

VENEZUELA

PANAMA

COLOMBIA

TRINIDAD AND TOBAGO

GUYANA

SURINAME

FRENCH GUIANA (Fr.)

SIERRA LEONE

LIBERIA

N

0° Equator

KIRIBATI

W E

Galapagos Islands
(Ecuador)

ECUADOR

Amazon

OCEAN

S

PERU

BRAZIL

OCEA

G SAMOA

Lima

15° AMERICAN
SAMOA
(U.S.)

TONGA

COOK
ISLANDS
(N.Z.)

FRENCH POLYNESIA
(Fr.)

BOLIVIA

Brasília

Rio de Janeiro

H Tropic of Capricorn

Easter Island
(Chile)

PARAGUAY

30° International Date Line

ARGENTINA

URUGUAY

Santiago

Buenos
Aires

I

45°

World Political Map

⊙ National capital

• Major city

— International boundary

FALKLAND IS.
(U.K.)

South
Georgia
(U.K.)

J 0   1000   2000 Miles

0   1000   2000   3000 Kilometers

South
Orkney Is.
(U.K.)

60°

South
Shetland Is.
(U.K.)

Weddell
Sea

K Antarctic Circle

SOUTHERN OCEAN

75°

L

180° **1** 165° **2** 150° **3** 135° **4** 120° **5** 105° **6** 90° **7** 75° **8** 60° **9** 45° **10** 30° **11** 1

ARCTIC OCEAN

A

75°

Franz Josef Land

B

Novaya Zemlya

60°

Sea of Okhotsk

R U S S I A

Bering Sea

C

FINLAND

SWEDEN

Moscow

Novosibirsk

45°

International Date Line

EST.
LAT.
LITH.
POLAND
BELARUS

Volga

KAZAKHSTAN

MONGOLIA

GERMANY

UKRAINE

UZBEKISTAN

KYRG

NORTH KOREA

Sea of Japan

D

AUS.
HUNG.
ROM.
MOLD.

Black Sea

GEO.
ARM. AZER.
TURKMENISTAN

TAJIK.

Beijing

Seoul SOUTH KOREA

JAPAN
Tōkyō

30°

CZ.
BOS.
SERB.
BUL.
ALB.

GREECE

TURKEY

Tehrān

AFGHANISTAN

C H I N A

Yangtze

Shanghai

Crete

CYPRUS
LEB.
ISRAEL
SYRIA

JORDAN

IRAQ

IRAN

KUWAIT

NEPAL

BHU.

PACIFIC

Tropic of Cancer

E

Mediterranean Sea

TUNISIA

Cairo

QATAR

PAKISTAN

Karachi

Ganges

Kolkata
(Calcutta)

BNG.

30°

LIBYA

EGYPT

SAUDI ARABIA

U.A.E.

OMAN

Mumbai
(Bombay)

INDIA

MYANMAR

LAOS

TAIWAN

Hong Kong

NORTHERN MARIANA ISLANDS
(U.S.)

WAKE ISLAND
(U.S.)

15°

NIGER

Red Sea

YEMEN

Arabian Sea

Bay of Bengal

THAILAND

South China Sea

O C E A N

CHAD

SUDAN

ERITREA

Addis
Ababa

DJIBOUTI

Bangkok

CAMBODIA

VIETNAM

PHILIPPINES

Manila

GUAM
(U.S.)

F

NIGERIA

CENTRAL
AFRICAN
REPUBLIC

CAMEROON

Congo

ETHIOPIA

SOMALIA

SRI LANKA

MALDIVES

BRUNEI

MALAYSIA

PALAU

FED. STATES OF
MICRONESIA

MARSHALL
ISLANDS

GABON

CONGO

UGANDA

KENYA

SINGAPORE

Borneo

15°

EQUATORIAL

RWANDA
DEM. REP.
OF THE CONGO
BURUNDI

SEYCHELLES

Sumatra

Jakarta

Java

INDONESIA

New Guinea

PAPUA
NEW GUINEA

**SOLOMON
ISLANDS**

Equator

0°

TANZANIA

EAST TIMOR

G

ANGOLA

MALAWI

COMOROS

I N D I A N

15°

ZAMBIA

ZIMBABWE

MOZAMBIQUE

MADAGASCAR

MAURITIUS

Coral Sea

VANUATU

NEW CALEDONIA
(Fr.)

FIJI

NAMIBIA

BOTSWANA

*REUNION
(Fr.)*

Tropic of Capricorn

H

Johannesburg

AUSTRALIA

Brisbane

**SOUTH
AFRICA**

SWAZILAND

LESOTHO

O C E A N

Perth

Darling

Sydney

30°

Melbourne

Auckland

NEW ZEALAND

I

Tasmania

*Îles Kerguélen
(Fr.)*

45°

J

S O U T H E R N   O C E A N

60°

Antarctic Circle

K

75°

A N T A R C T I C A

© Rand McNally & Co.
Made in U.S.A.
N-CLA10000-P1- -9-9-11

L

Global Perspectives

The United States developed relatively isolated from other major world powers. It is separated from Europe by the Atlantic Ocean and from Asia by the Pacific Ocean. The colonies that became Canada were small and widely separated. The center of Mexico, which the United States defeated in a war, was far away across a desert. Nevertheless, the United States has always had some connections with the rest of the world. The American Revolution was part of a series of revolutions that affected France and the rest of Europe and Latin America.

Today, with increasing communications and faster transportation, the United States is even more connected to the rest of the world. Americans trade with many countries in order to sell goods and services and to import vital fuels and other raw materials. Conflicts in the Middle East, where three continents, three religions, and several culture groups all come together, have become especially intense. During the Cold War, this region was a borderland between the center of communism in the Soviet Union and countries that were non-communist, led by the United States. Since the end of the Cold War, terrorist groups that are not under the government of any one country have emerged as powerful forces. Some of these groups use Islam as their identity, although all religions teach peace and international understanding as the best way for people to live. Many of the Middle Eastern countries have rapidly growing populations and problems providing high standards of living for their people. Such conditions foster the growth of extremist and terrorist groups.

© Craig DeBourbon/SSG C. A. DeBourbon/iStock

▲ *In 2003, American forces invaded Iraq to remove Saddam Hussein from power.*

Did You Know

?

Although Christianity has more followers than any other religion (2 billion) and is growing at a rate of 1.5 percent per year, Islam with 1.3 billion followers is growing the fastest: an estimated 2.9 percent per year.

	1776	1905	1918
People	Benjamin Franklin goes to France as an official representative of the Second Continental Congress.	Theodore Roosevelt helps negotiate the Treaty of Portsmouth, ending the Russo-Japanese War in Asia.	To prevent another war, Woodrow Wilson proposes to include Fourteen Points in the Treaty of Versailles ending World War I.
	1784	1898	1914
Events	The ship *Empress of China* sails loaded with goods to begin trade with China.	The Spanish-American War results in U.S. possession of the Philippines, Puerto Rico, Guam, and Cuba.	The Panama Canal, built by the United States, opens to ships.
	1851	1882	1906
Literature	Herman Melville's *Moby Dick* is published, telling the story of American whaling in far-away oceans.	Mark Twain publishes *The Prince and the Pauper*, which takes place in sixteenth-century England.	Upton Sinclair publishes *The Jung* about immigrants working in the meatpacking industry in Chicago.

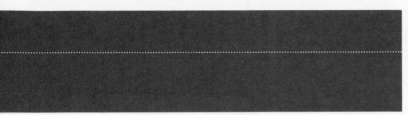

Within the United States, too, the pattern of population distribution is changing. Since the end of World War II, many Americans have been attracted by warmer weather to the South and the West, which make up the Sun Belt. These regions are also rich in resources, making them attractive to industry. Companies have built new factories and offices in the Sun Belt, and these jobs are an additional attraction. Retired people have moved there in large numbers to enjoy the warm climate. At the same time, immigrants from Latin America have settled in the Sun Belt, which is the closest part of the United States to their former homeland.

▲ *Dallas, Texas, is one of the largest cities in the Sun Belt.*

U.S. Imports and Exports, 1960–2005

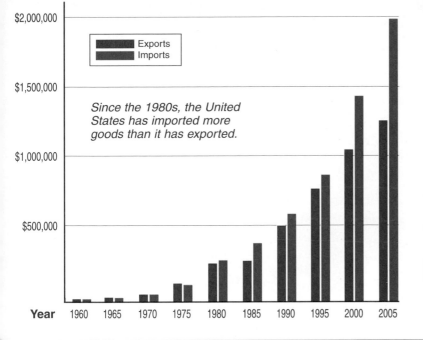

Legend: Exports, Imports

Since the 1980s, the United States has imported more goods than it has exported.

U.S. Oil Imports, 1975–2005

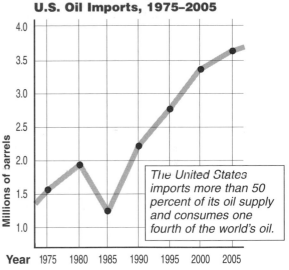

Millions of barrels

The United States imports more than 50 percent of its oil supply and consumes one fourth of the world's oil.

1950
Ralph Bunche wins the Nobel Peace Prize for his role as mediator during the Arab-Israeli War.

1961
Sargent Shriver is appointed by John F. Kennedy to be the first director of the Peace Corps.

1972
Richard Nixon becomes the first U.S. president to visit China while in office.

1945
The United Nations charter is adopted by representatives from 50 countries meeting in San Francisco.

1973
The United States withdraws all of its troops from Vietnam, ending U.S. involvement in the Vietnam War.

2002
Following terrorist attacks on New York and Washington, the U.S. sends forces to overthrow Afghanistan's Taliban government.

1958
The Ugly American by William J. Lederer and Eugene Burdick tells of arrogance and incompetence by American personnel in Southeast Asia.

1989
Amy Tan publishes *The Joy Luck Club*, which tells about life of Chinese Americans both before and after they come to America.

1990
The Things They Carried, by Tim O'Brien, tells the story of an American platoon in Vietnam during the Vietnam War.

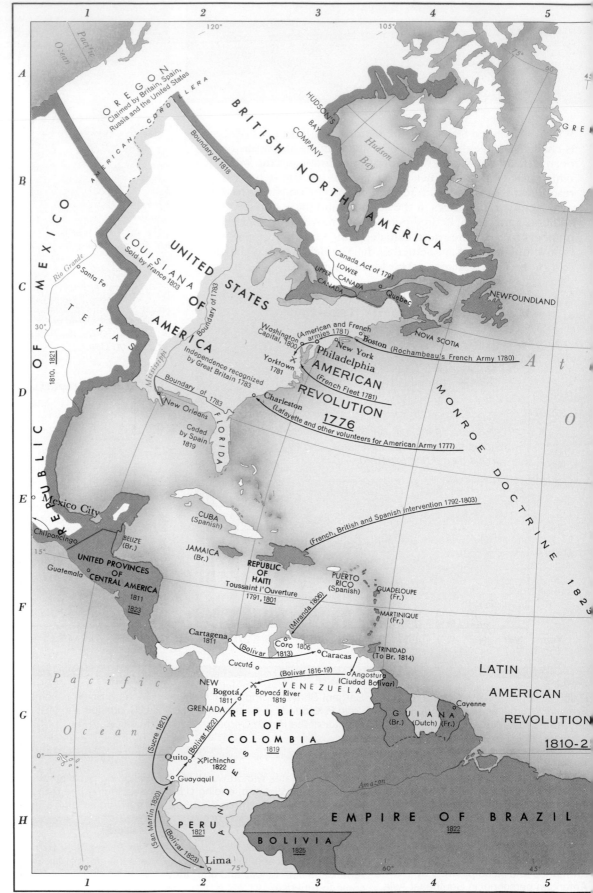

OREGON
Claimed by Britain, Spain,
Russia and the United States

AMERICAN CORDILLERA

Boundary of 1818

BRITISH NORTH AMERICA

HUDSON'S BAY COMPANY

Hudson Bay

GREE

UNITED STATES OF AMERICA

LOUISIANA
Sold by France 1803

REPUBLIC OF MEXICO

Rio Grande

Santa Fe

TEXAS

30°

1810, 1821

Boundary of 1783

Mississippi

Canada Act of 1791

LOWER CANADA

UPPER CANADA

Quebec

NOVA SCOTIA

NEWFOUNDLAND

Washington
Capital, 1800

(American and French
armies 1781)

Boston
(Rochambeau's French Army 1780)

New York

Philadelphia

AMERICAN

(French Fleet 1781)

REVOLUTION

Yorktown
1781

1776

Independence recognized
by Great Britain 1783

Boundary of 1783

New Orleans

Charleston
(Lafayette and other volunteers for American Army 1777)

MONROE DOCTRINE 1823

Atl

O

Ceded
by Spain
1819

FLORIDA

CUBA
(Spanish)

JAMAICA
(Br.)

(French, British and Spanish intervention 1792-1803)

Mexico City

Chilpancingo

BELIZE
(Br.)

UNITED PROVINCES
OF
CENTRAL AMERICA
1811
1823

Guatemala

15°

REPUBLIC
OF
HAITI
Toussaint l'Ouverture
1791, **1801**

PUERTO
RICO
(Spanish)

GUADELOUPE
(Fr.)

MARTINIQUE
(Fr.)

Pacific

Ocean

Cartagena
1811

(Bolivar)

Cucutá

Coro 1806
(Bolivar 1813)

Caracas

(Miranda 1806)

TRINIDAD
(To Br. 1814)

(Bolivar 1816-19)

Angostura
(Ciudad Bolivar)

LATIN

AMERICAN

REVOLUTION

1810-2

NEW

Bogotá
1811

GRENADA

Boyacá River
1819

VENEZUELA

REPUBLIC
OF
COLOMBIA
1819

GUIANA
(Br.) (Dutch) (Fr.)

Cayenne

ANDES

(Sucre 1821)

(Bolivar 1822)

Quito

Pichincha
1822

Guayaquil

0°

(San Martin 1820)

(Bolivar 1823)

PERU
1821

Amazon

EMPIRE OF BRAZIL
1822

BOLIVIA
1825

Lima

90°

75°

60°

45°

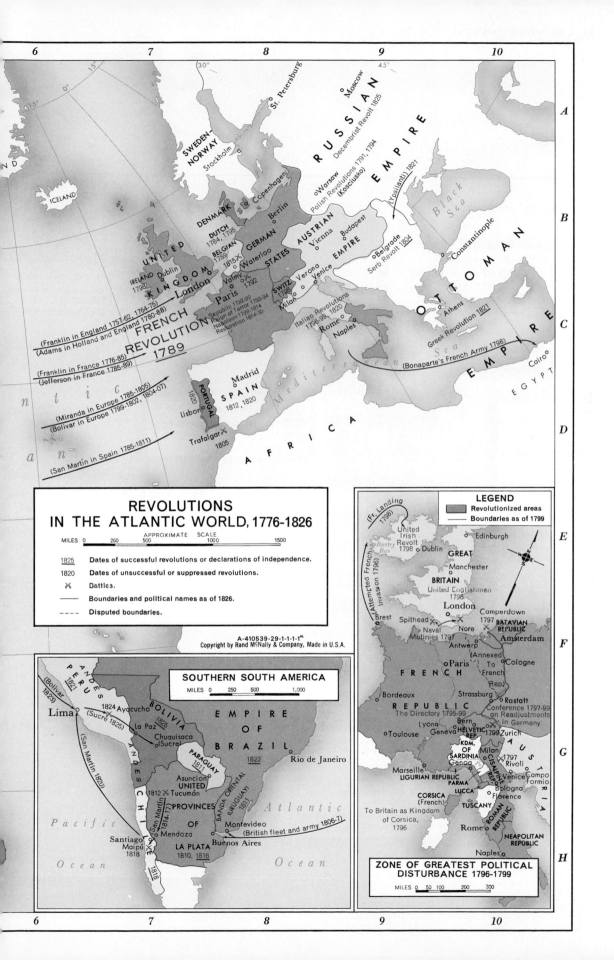

REVOLUTIONS IN THE ATLANTIC WORLD, 1776-1826

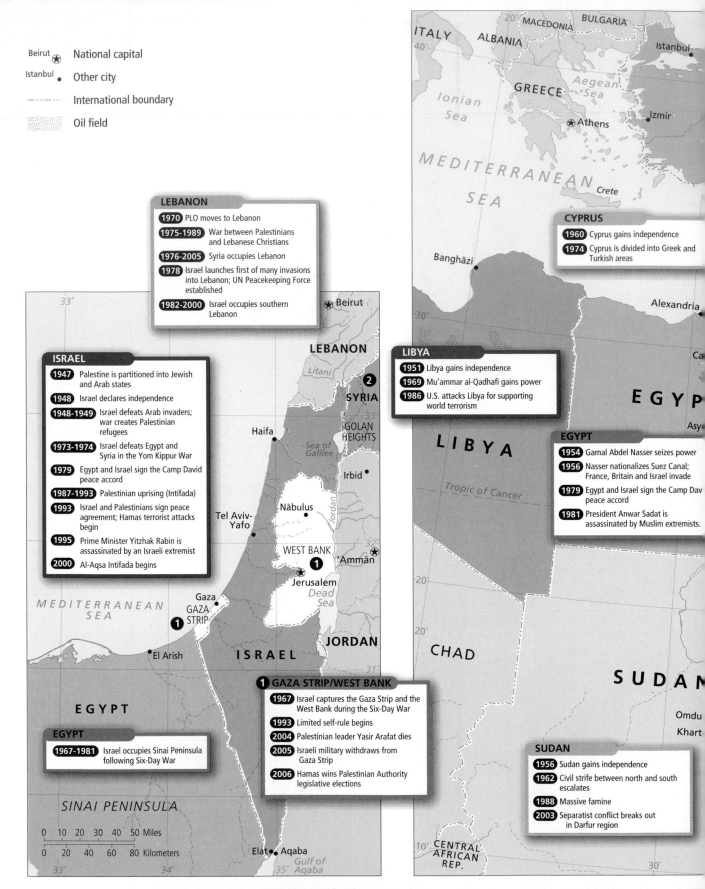

Beirut ⊛ National capital

Istanbul • Other city

‒ ‒ ‒ ‒ ‒ International boundary

▒▒▒ Oil field

LEBANON

1970 PLO moves to Lebanon

1975-1989 War between Palestinians and Lebanese Christians

1976-2005 Syria occupies Lebanon

1978 Israel launches first of many invasions into Lebanon; UN Peacekeeping Force established

1982-2000 Israel occupies southern Lebanon

CYPRUS

1960 Cyprus gains independence

1974 Cyprus is divided into Greek and Turkish areas

ISRAEL

1947 Palestine is partitioned into Jewish and Arab states

1948 Israel declares independence

1948-1949 Israel defeats Arab invaders; war creates Palestinian refugees

1973-1974 Israel defeats Egypt and Syria in the Yom Kippur War

1979 Egypt and Israel sign the Camp David peace accord

1987-1993 Palestinian uprising (Intifada)

1993 Israel and Palestinians sign peace agreement; Hamas terrorist attacks begin

1995 Prime Minister Yitzhak Rabin is assassinated by an Israeli extremist

2000 Al-Aqsa Intifada begins

LIBYA

1951 Libya gains independence

1969 Mu'ammar al-Qadhafi gains power

1986 U.S. attacks Libya for supporting world terrorism

EGYPT

1954 Gamal Abdel Nasser seizes power

1956 Nasser nationalizes Suez Canal; France, Britain and Israel invade

1979 Egypt and Israel sign the Camp David peace accord

1981 President Anwar Sadat is assassinated by Muslim extremists.

EGYPT

1967-1981 Israel occupies Sinai Peninsula following Six-Day War

① GAZA STRIP/WEST BANK

1967 Israel captures the Gaza Strip and the West Bank during the Six-Day War

1993 Limited self-rule begins

2004 Palestinian leader Yasir Arafat dies

2005 Israeli military withdraws from Gaza Strip

2006 Hamas wins Palestinian Authority legislative elections

SUDAN

1956 Sudan gains independence

1962 Civil strife between north and south escalates

1988 Massive famine

2003 Separatist conflict breaks out in Darfur region

0 10 20 30 40 50 Miles

0 20 40 60 80 Kilometers

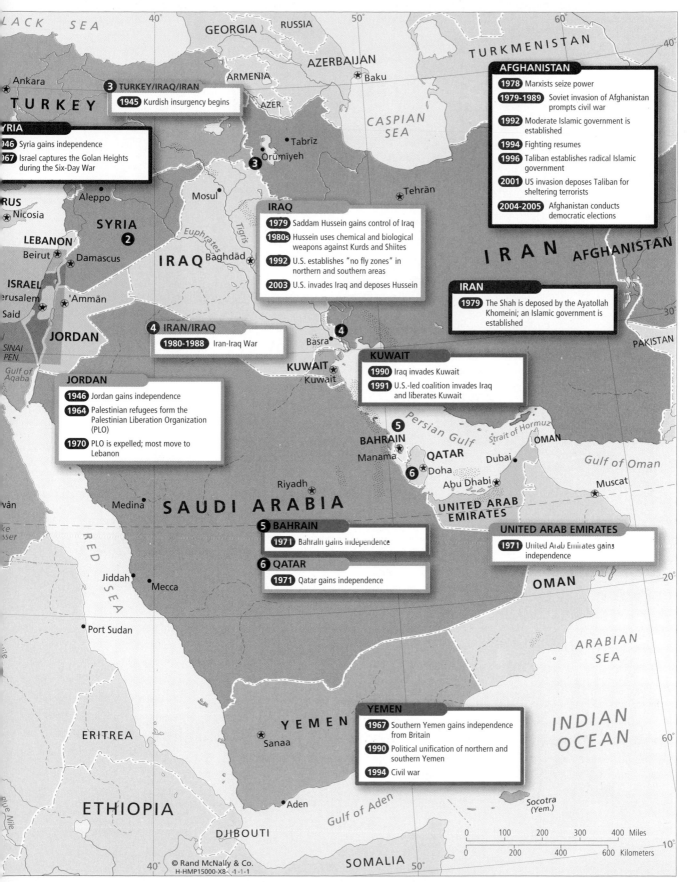

AFGHANISTAN
- **1978** Marxists seize power
- **1979-1989** Soviet invasion of Afghanistan prompts civil war
- **1992** Moderate Islamic government is established
- **1994** Fighting resumes
- **1996** Taliban establishes radical Islamic government
- **2001** US invasion deposes Taliban for sheltering terrorists
- **2004-2005** Afghanistan conducts democratic elections

3 TURKEY/IRAQ/IRAN
- **1945** Kurdish insurgency begins

SYRIA
- **946** Syria gains independence
- **067** Israel captures the Golan Heights during the Six-Day War

IRAQ
- **1979** Saddam Hussein gains control of Iraq
- **1980s** Hussein uses chemical and biological weapons against Kurds and Shiites
- **1992** U.S. establishes "no fly zones" in northern and southern areas
- **2003** U.S. invades Iraq and deposes Hussein

IRAN
- **1979** The Shah is deposed by the Ayatollah Khomeini; an Islamic government is established

4 IRAN/IRAQ
- **1980-1988** Iran-Iraq War

KUWAIT
- **1990** Iraq invades Kuwait
- **1991** U.S.-led coalition invades Iraq and liberates Kuwait

JORDAN
- **1946** Jordan gains independence
- **1964** Palestinian refugees form the Palestinian Liberation Organization (PLO)
- **1970** PLO is expelled; most move to Lebanon

5 BAHRAIN
- **1971** Bahrain gains independence

6 QATAR
- **1971** Qatar gains independence

UNITED ARAB EMIRATES
- **1971** United Arab Emirates gains independence

YEMEN
- **1967** Southern Yemen gains independence from Britain
- **1990** Political unification of northern and southern Yemen
- **1994** Civil war

© Rand McNally & Co.
H-HMP15000-X8- -1-1-1

0 100 200 300 400 Miles
0 200 400 600 Kilometers

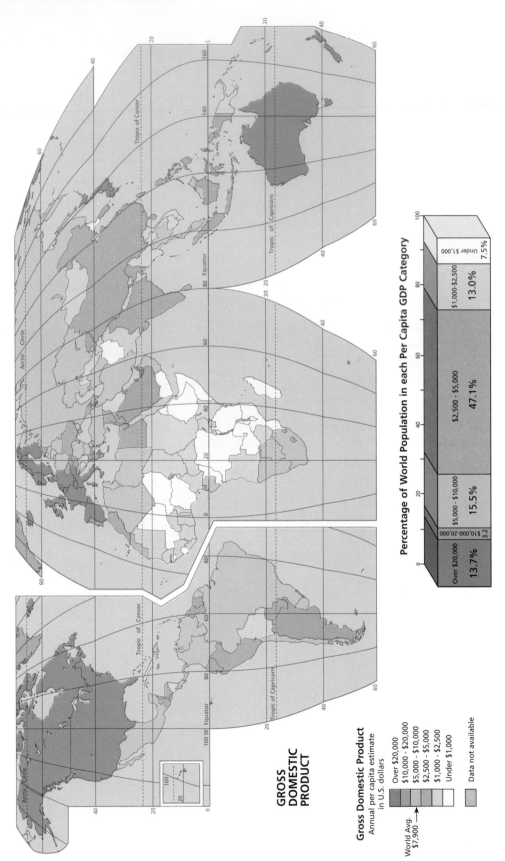

Percentage of World Population in each Per Capita GDP Category

Over $20,000	$10,000-20,000	$5,000 - $10,000	$2,500 - $5,000	$1,000-$2,500	Under $1,000
13.7%	3.2	15.5%	47.1%	13.0%	7.5%

GROSS DOMESTIC PRODUCT

Gross Domestic Product
Annual per capita estimate
in U.S. dollars

World Avg. — $7,900

Over $20,000
$10,000 - $20,000
$5,000 - $10,000
$2,500 - $5,000
$1,000 - $2,500
Under $1,000

Data not available

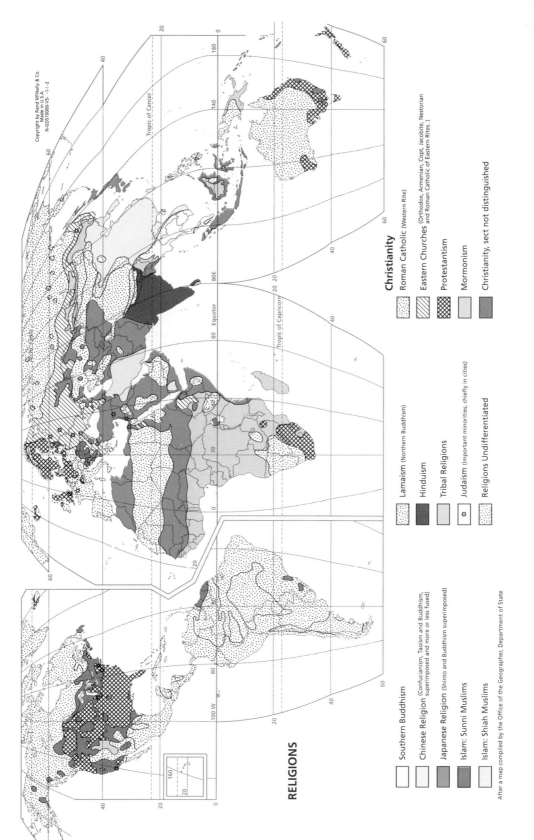

RELIGIONS

Southern Buddhism

Chinese Religion (Confucianism, Taoism and Buddhism, superimposed and more or less fused)

Japanese Religion (Shinto and Buddhism superimposed)

Islam: Sunni Muslims

Islam: Shiah Muslims

Lamaism (Northern Buddhism)

Hinduism

Tribal Religions

Judaism (Important minorities, chiefly in cities)

Religions Undifferentiated

Christianity

Roman Catholic (Western Rite)

Eastern Churches (Orthodox, Armenian, Copt, Jacobite, Nestorian and Roman Catholic of Eastern Rites.)

Protestantism

Mormonism

Christianity, sect not distinguished

After a map compiled by the Office of the Geographer, Department of State

Copyright by Rand McNally & Co.
Made in U.S.A.
N-GD510000-VS--1-1.-2

Tropic of Cancer

Equator

Tropic of Capricorn

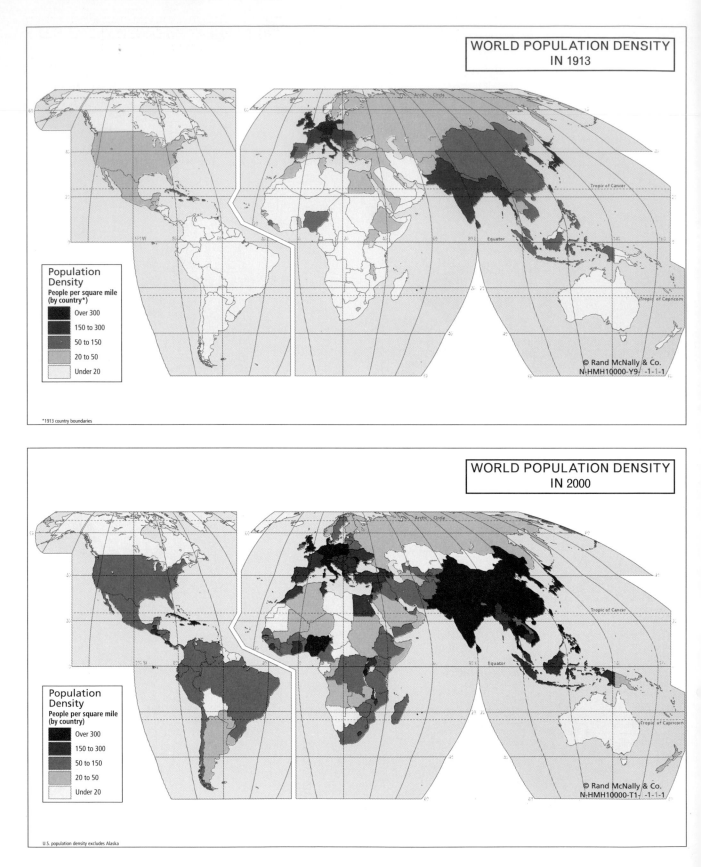

WORLD POPULATION DENSITY
IN 1913

Population
Density
**People per square mile
(by country*)**

- Over 300
- 150 to 300
- 50 to 150
- 20 to 50
- Under 20

© Rand McNally & Co.
N-HMH10000-Y9- -1-1-1

*1913 country boundaries

WORLD POPULATION DENSITY
IN 2000

Population
Density
**People per square mile
(by country)**

- Over 300
- 150 to 300
- 50 to 150
- 20 to 50
- Under 20

© Rand McNally & Co.
N-HMH10000-T1- -1-1-1

U.S. population density excludes Alaska

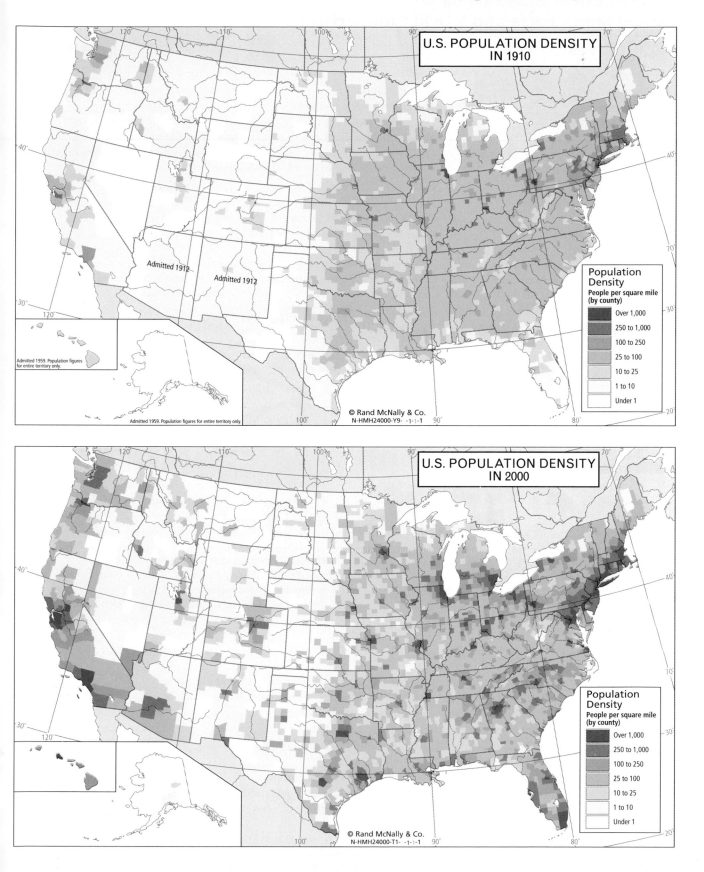

U.S. POPULATION DENSITY IN 1910

Admitted 1912

Admitted 1912

Admitted 1959. Population figures for entire territory only.

Admitted 1959. Population figures for entire territory only.

© Rand McNally & Co.
N-HMH24000-Y9- -1-1-1

Population Density
People per square mile (by county)

- Over 1,000
- 250 to 1,000
- 100 to 250
- 25 to 100
- 10 to 25
- 1 to 10
- Under 1

U.S. POPULATION DENSITY IN 2000

© Rand McNally & Co.
N-HMH24000-T1- -1-1-1

Population Density
People per square mile (by county)

- Over 1,000
- 250 to 1,000
- 100 to 250
- 25 to 100
- 10 to 25
- 1 to 10
- Under 1

United States Facts and World Comparisons

Superlatives

Largest state in size	Alaska	663,267 sq. mi.
Smallest state in size	Rhode Island	1,545 sq. mi.
Highest point	Mount McKinley (Alaska)	20,320 ft.
Lowest point	Death Valley (California)	282 ft. below sea level
Longest river	Mississippi-Missouri	3,710 mi.
Largest lake in size/volume of water	Lake Michigan	22,300 sq. mi./1,200 cu. mi.
Deepest lake	Crater Lake (Oregon)	1,932 ft
Northernmost point	Point Barrow (Alaska)	71°N, 156°W
Southernmost point	Ka Lae (Hawaii)	19°N, 156°W
Easternmost point	West Quoddy Head (Maine)	45°N, 67°W
Westernmost point	Cape Wrangell, Attu Island (Alaska)	53°N, 172°E

World Comparison • Mount Everest (Tibet and Nepal) is the highest mountain in the world. It rises about 29,028 feet above sea level. Mauna Kea (Hawaii) is the tallest mountain in world. Its base is on the bottom of the Pacific Ocean. It rises 33,476 feet, but only 13,796 feet is above sea level.

Top Ten Cities in 1900 and 2000

Largest U.S. Cities in Population (1900)

1	New York, NY	3,437,000
2	Chicago, IL	1,699,000
3	Philadelphia, PA	1,294,000
4	St. Louis, MO	575,000
5	Boston, MA	561,000
6	Baltimore, MD	509,000
7	Cleveland, OH	382,000
8	Buffalo, NY	352,000
9	San Francisco, CA	343,000
10	Cincinnati, OH	326,000

World Comparison • The population of New York, NY, reached 1 million in the late 1800s. Rome, Italy, is believed to have had 1 million people around 200 B.C.

Largest U.S. Cities in Population (Metropolitan Population — 2000)

1	New York, NY	21,200,000
2	Los Angeles, CA	16,374,000
3	Chicago, IL	9,158,000
4	Washington, DC	7,608,000
5	San Francisco, CA	7,039,000
6	Philadelphia, PA	6,188,000
7	Boston, MA	5,819,000
8	Detroit, MI	5,456,000
9	Dallas, TX	5,222,000
10	Houston, TX	4,670,000

World Comparison • In 2000, New York ranked fourth among the world's largest cities in population. Tokyo, Japan (26,444,000) was the largest, followed by Mexico City, Mexico and São Paulo, Brazil.

Developments in U.S. Transportation

1756	Stagecoach lines operate between Boston, New York, Baltimore, and Philadelphia.
1807	Steamboats carry passengers on the Hudson River between New York and Albany.
1830	Steam-powered train service begins between Charleston and Hamburg, SC.
1869	Transcontinental railroad is completed across United States.
1913	Ford factory in Highland Park, MI, turns out Model T automobiles on an assembly line.
1920s	Passenger airlines begin operating in United States.
1956	The Interstate Highway System construction project is launched.
1976	Supersonic airline passenger travel begins between New York and London (ends in 2003).
2000	North America's first high-speed "bullet" train service begins between New York and Boston.

World Comparison • In the 1660s, Paris began operating a coach line that carried passengers around the city in horse-drawn carriages. Today the TGV (a train that travels between Paris and other cities in Western Europe) is the world's fastest passenger train. It travels at a speed of 186 miles per hour.

U.S. Presidents and Geography Connections

President	Years in Office	Geography Connection
1. George Washington	1789–1797	Number of states increases from 11 to 16.
2. John Adams	1797–1801	Washington, D.C., becomes the national capital.
3. Thomas Jefferson	1801–1809	Louisiana Purchase nearly doubles size of United States.
4. James Madison	1809–1817	War against Great Britain is fought on U.S. soil.
5. James Monroe	1817–1825	United States gains Florida from Spain.
6. John Quincy Adams	1825–1829	Erie Canal provides link from Great Lakes to Atlantic Ocean.
7. Andrew Jackson	1829–1837	Arkansas and Michigan become states.
8. Martin Van Buren	1837–1841	Cherokees are forced to move west of the Mississippi River.
9. William H. Harrison	1841	(Harrison dies one month after taking office.)
10. John Tyler	1841–1845	Texas becomes part of the United States.
11. James K. Polk	1845–1849	U.S. boundaries extend to the Pacific Coast.
12. Zachary Taylor	1849–1850	Gold rush brings thousands of people to California.
13. Millard Fillmore	1850–1853	California becomes a state.
14. Franklin Pierce	1853–1857	United States buys land in the southwest from Mexico.
15. James Buchanan	1857–1861	Six southern states secede.
16. Abraham Lincoln	1861–1865	Civil War divides the nation.
17. Andrew Johnson	1865–1869	United States buys Alaska.
18. Ulysses S. Grant	1869–1877	First coast-to-coast railroad is completed.
19. Rutherford B. Hayes	1877–1881	Yellowstone becomes first national park.
20. James A. Garfield	1881	(Garfield dies a few months after taking office.)
21. Chester A. Arthur	1881–1885	Brooklyn Bridge is built between Brooklyn and Manhattan.
22. Grover Cleveland	1885–1889	Statue of Liberty is dedicated in New York Harbor.
23. Benjamin Harrison	1889–1893	Six states enter the Union.
24. Grover Cleveland	1893–1897	Utah becomes a state.
25. William McKinley	1897–1901	United States gains first overseas possessions.
26. Theodore Roosevelt	1901–1909	United States gains Panama Canal Zone.
27. William H. Taft	1909–1913	New Mexico and Arizona become final mainland states.
28. Woodrow Wilson	1913–1921	Coast-to-coast telephone service is established.
29. Warren G. Harding	1921–1923	Congress sets limits on immigration.
30. Calvin Coolidge	1923–1929	U.S. highway 66 connects Chicago and Los Angeles.
31. Herbert C. Hoover	1929–1933	World's tallest skyscraper is built in New York, New York.
32. Franklin D. Roosevelt	1933–1945	Dust storms destroy land in the Great Plains.
33. Harry S. Truman	1945–1953	Puerto Rico becomes a self-governing commonwealth.
34. Dwight D. Eisenhower	1953–1961	Alaska and Hawaii become states.
35. John F. Kennedy	1961–1963	Civil rights supporters march on Washington, D.C.
36. Lyndon B. Johnson	1963–1969	Gateway Arch is built in St. Louis, Missouri.
37. Richard M. Nixon	1969–1974	Congress grants 44 million acres in Alaska to native peoples.
38. Gerald R. Ford	1974–1977	United States commemorates its bicentennial.
39. Jimmy Carter	1977–1981	Eruption of Mount St. Helens causes damage in Washington.
40. Ronald W. Reagan	1981–1989	Fires destroy much of Yellowstone National Park.
41. George H.W. Bush	1989–1993	Largest oil spill in U.S. waters occurs off Alaska's coast.
42. William J. Clinton	1993–2001	United States gives control of Panama Canal to Panama.
43. George W. Bush	2001-	Terrorists destroy World Trade Center in New York.

In addition to place names that appear on the maps in this atlas, the Index also lists names of people, groups, events, and other topics related to American history. It provides explanatory information, such as dates, identifications, and geographic locations for many entries. When appropriate, entries are cross-referenced to related topics.

The Index lists boldfaced page numbers on which each entry appears. A small letter beside a page number identifies a specific map on the page on which the entry appears. Postal abbreviations are used for state names.

The following abbreviations also are used:

Ft.	Fort	St.	Saint
g	graph	t	table
Is.	Islands	terr.	territory
p	photograph	U.S.	United States
pop.	population		